Praise for *M* 〔barcode: 10661914〕

When I picked this book up, I simply could not put it down. So many emotions ran through me as I read it. I struggle even now to find the right words to describe them. Grief. Sadness. Despair. Tragedy. Heartbroken. Thankful. Blessed. Wisdom. Perseverance. Hope! Yes, there is hope on the other side of suicide, and it is found in Christ and the rock solid promises of His Word. This was a painful book for my friend Frank Page to write. But it is a book that will minister to thousands of souls who have walked the dark path of death to find there is light and life on the other side. This book is brutal in its honesty. That is why it is so powerful. Thank you, my friend, for opening up your heart. Melissa's death is not in vain.

Daniel L. Akin, President
Southeastern Baptist Theological Seminary

Although my four children are grown and I am a very proud grandfather, my greatest fear is still losing one of my children. I do not know how I would cope with the death of a child, especially death by suicide. Dr. Page has experienced my worst fear and has mustered the courage and wisdom to help rescue and restore others who are living in this suffocating darkness. *Melissa* will give hope and comfort to those who are living with the pain of suicide, and perhaps even more important, save others from this pain by shining light on the signs, symptoms, and solutions to self-destructive behavior.

Jim DeMint
President, The Heritage Foundation
U.S. Senator 2005–2013

Painful . . . Poignant . . . Penetrating . . . Powerful. These words, along with a host of other moving and emotional descriptors, continually came to mind as I was turning the pages in this transparent portrayal of the struggles faced by Frank Page and his family following the suicide of his adult daughter Melissa. It is anything but a simplistic "how to" manual for dealing with grief and loss. Frank Page walks us through the reality of his struggles in an authentic manner that allows the readers to experience with him the hurts that accompany such a traumatic interruption in one's life and family. The book, however, is not just the telling of a personal story. Rather, it is a pastoral and fatherly reflection, grounded in the love and mercy of God as revealed in holy Scripture, intended to provide guidance for families and individuals who have walked down the paths of sorrow that the author himself has walked. Even beyond this valuable contribution, the book offers helpful and wise counsel in a tender, compassionate, and hopeful way for those struggling with doubt, depression, disillusionment, and thoughts of suicide. I am truly grateful for Frank Page's courageous efforts to write this powerful book. Without a doubt, this work was hard for him to write . . . and at times, it is a hard book to read. Yet it is a book that needed to be written and, moreover, a book that needs to be read.

David S. Dockery
President, Union University

The hardest day of my life as a minister was when the call came that a dear friend and deacon's son had just killed himself. I never dreaded a visit more than I did that one. What could I say? How could I possibly know how they feel? I wish I had possessed Frank Page's book back then that you hold in your hands now! The author is one of the finest preacher/scholars in our Convention.

He is articulate and passionate. He occupies one of the highest offices in Southern Baptist life. But never would I have imagined that he would have opened his heart and soul with us about his daughter's suicide as he has in these pages. You will experience the heart throbbing passion of grief and the guilt and frustration that a parent experiences when a child chooses suicide. You will not want to put this book down until you complete it. You will experience blessing, inspiration, the agony of grief, and the clear sufficiency of our Lord.

James T. (Jimmy) Draper
President Emeritus, LifeWay Christian Resources

Heartbroken . . . Painful . . . Hopeful . . . Helpful. From this kind heart to your heart, Frank Page has poured himself out word by word with transparency about suffering in life. With a healing heart and limping with pain, he wants to help all of us. This book will help you, so read it. This book will help others, so share it. It is a moving story that will move you and others just like it moved me.

Dr. Ronnie Floyd
Senior Pastor, Cross Church, Springdale, Arkansas

Death by suicide: a heart wrenching term for any parent to hear about their child, even more devastating given the close bonds between "Daddy's little girl" and her father. I clearly witnessed this devastation firsthand as I stood beside my good friend Frank Page at his daughter Melissa's grave. How do we deal with that kind of tragedy? In this book, *Melissa*, Frank not only deals with these black holes of grief and despair, but also provides an answer for the even larger question of how we deal with life and so many of the problems even the strongest Christians can encounter. Christ is the answer, the only answer. Frank paints a vivid portrait of a God who loved us so much he gave his son for us. A loving God who provides for us even in the terror of "the shadow of death."

Major General Gary L. Harrell, USA (Ret.)

These words are not a mere theoretical treatise but have been beaten out and written out on the anvil of personal experience by Frank Page. He writes to us out of a heart of love not only for Melissa but for us . . . and for anyone anywhere who may be contemplating crashing the gates of heaven on their own initiative. Hope and healing come with every passing page. Read it and reap!

O. S. Hawkins, President/CEO
GuideStone Financial Resources

I prefer to read books by authors that have been there. Frank Page has walked through the valley and now offers us help from his journey.

Johnny Hunt, Pastor
First Baptist Woodstock, Georgia

I attended the funeral. The pain and questioning were a thick fog. But through it all the faith and stamina of Frank Page came shining through. He knows whereof he speaks. Read and be blessed, and be a blessing to many others going through the same valley.

John Marshall, Pastor
Second Baptist Church, Springfield, Missouri

Never again will I see Frank Page the same way. Never again will I see anyone the same way. *Melissa* opens the heart of a leader to the love, pain, hope, despair, joy, sorrow, and ultimate peace that God in His providence allows. He invites us all in to this very tender place. He does not hide the most personal reflections and feelings.

And he does it for our sakes. You will weep. You will smile. You will thank God for His peace. And you will keep this book on hand to give to those who must walk a similarly lonely road. Thank you, Frank Page, for capturing your sorrow for our edification.

Paige Patterson, President
Southwestern Baptist Theological Seminary

Melissa is a heart-rending yet hope-inspiring story from the pen of parent/pastor Frank Page. As a parent, Page walks the reader through the passion of loving a child unconditionally, the pain of the most devastating loss, and the perseverance of a saint who knows "in whom He has believed." As a pastor, his heart's sensitivity is juxtaposed with heaven's hope, and he weaves these together with the help that hurting families are desperately seeking. In his theology of grief, Page walks hurting families through the bittersweet life in a fallen world. Rebellion against moral and spiritual values, drugs, depression, cancer, and suicide—these are Satan's weapons for throwing entire families into the darkest arena of spiritual warfare, and yet Page draws upon an effective divine arsenal that leads to spiritual victories and helps to preserve and celebrate the memories of God's goodness hidden even in the dark corners of life. This volume will inspire and instruct; it will move your focus from loneliness and tragedy to comfort and hope.

Dorothy Kelley Patterson
Professor of Theology in Women's Studies
Southwestern Baptist Theological Seminary

Stunning. Heart-wrenching. Gospel-centered. Breathtaking. I am struggling to articulate exactly what I want to say about this book. Frank Page raises a troubled child. He goes through the heartbreak of numerous issues with her. Then, when her life seemed to be on the mend, she learns she has cancer. Ultimately and tragically, even after the battle with cancer is won, she takes her life. As a father, I cannot begin to imagine the pain Frank and his wife, Dayle, are experiencing. As a reader, I know that I have seen God's grace and love poured out abundantly through this book. Simply stated, this book is one of the most powerful I've ever read.

Thom S. Rainer, President and CEO
LifeWay Christian Resources

This book comes straight from a father's heart that was devastated by the self-inflicted death of his irreplaceably precious daughter, Melissa. Motivated by his profound desire to be an instrument of healing and a passionate desire to reach those who are contemplating suicide, Frank Page was willing to revisit with excruciating transparency the waves of lostness, regret, embarrassment, grief, and anguish that he and his family have experienced. The readers will find in this book a tender sensitivity, empathetic understanding, biblical counsel, and above all a powerful message of peace and hope based on the unshakable conviction that we can "cast our broken hearts on Jesus and simply trust that He understands, He forgives, He knows our limitations, and He loves us in every circumstance."

Daniel R. Sanchez, Professor of Missions
Southwestern Baptist Theological Seminary

Melissa is an excellent recommendation for any person who is experiencing life when it has gotten out of control. Dr. Page exemplifies a transparent heart when he shares with his readers the pain and darkness that overshadowed him and his family through the death of his daughter; and yet the compassion from his heart for others leaps from the pages. He points us to God as the ultimate and only solution, the One who holds back the water in the ocean and the seas, a God who will never die and is able to handle all situations we may encounter in this life.

James Dixon Jr., Pastor
El-Bethel Baptist Church, Fort Washington, Maryland

Dr. Page's experience as a pastor, leader, and father has prepared him to speak with authority on this heart-wrenching subject—suicide. It is a must-read for those who have been touched by this tragedy. Dr. Page's insight, sensitivity, and wisdom help to move us through suicide's aftermath, bringing comfort, encouragement, and insight to all who read these pages.

Kaye Miller
National WMU President, 2005–2010

You would imagine that serving as president of the Southern Baptist Convention would be Dr. Page's impact moment. Not so. The writing of *Melissa* and her story will have a more lasting impact on people than anything he does for the Southern Baptist Convention. Dr. Page has shown us the human side of ministry like no one before. He has allowed us to feel his struggles and victories during this chapter of his life. His unadorned story reveals the heart of a father's love for his daughter and an earthly father crying out as a son to his heavenly Father for understanding. I am sure you will be blessed by this book. It will minister in places you thought were barren and bring a rush of living water to the dry places of your life. It will also be an invaluable resource for you in dealing with the ministry of suicide prevention.

A. B. Vines Sr., Senior Pastor
New Seasons Church, Spring Valley, California

From the heart of a Christian father comes a most remarkable and unforgettable account of the life of his daughter and the reality of suicide. We are all in debt to Frank Page for sharing from his generous, grieving, and deeply convictional heart as he tells this story and helps us all to give thanks for the gift of life, even as we seek to celebrate and cherish this gift—and especially the gift of our children.

R. Albert Mohler Jr., President
Southern Baptist Theological Seminary

This book is raw, gritty, and tough. Most Christians have not been through the issues surrounding suicide like Frank was forced to do when his daughter took her own life. Or, I should probably say, most have not *felt* through the issues like he has. Reading this book felt often like a punch in the gut—but a healthy and necessary one. To respond to suicide as a Christian means to feel the pain deeply and move through it in Christ, not to sweep it away with simple answers. Frank is able to apply truths that all evangelicals *claim* to believe in an area that desperately needs that application. And he does it grippingly, weaving the story of Melissa in and out throughout the book. This book, while heartbreaking, is full of hope and answers for those who are struggling with the pain of depression or the sting of loss.

J. D. Greear, Lead Pastor
The Summit Church, Durham, North Carolina

Melissa is from the healing heart of a courageous father. Thank you, my friend, for giving us a glimpse of the radical redefinition of one's reality when tragedy strikes! You share the heart wrenching struggles of a suicide survivor who is sustained by the power and loving mercy of the living God! You teach us how to survive a paralyzing loss and celebrate a precious life. May the Lord bless you for your helpful, holy hints to pulpit and pew alike, as we minister to hurting hearts.

K. Marshall Williams Sr., Senior Pastor
Nazarene Baptist Church, Philadelphia, Pennsylvania
Vice President, National African American Fellowship, SBC

I have always respected and admired Dr. Frank Page. But my respect and admiration for him has risen to another level because of his book *Melissa*. To expose and write about something that many of us would want to keep private must have been extremely difficult for him. However, his primary purpose is that what the Page family went through will help other families who may go through the same experience. May you be blessed and encouraged as you read this inspirational book.

Fred Luter Jr.
President, Southern Baptist Convention
Pastor, Franklin Avenue Baptist Church, New Orleans, Louisiana

Melissa

978-1-4336-7910-0

Published by B&H Publishing Group
Nashville, Tennessee

Dewey Decimal Classification: 248.86
Subject Heading: SUICIDE \ BEREAVEMENT \
TEENAGERS—SUICIDE

Scripture is taken from Holman Christian Standard Bible®
(HCSB), copyright © 1999, 2000, 2002, 2003, 2009 by
Holman Bible Publishers. Used by permission. All rights
reserved. Also used: King James Version (KJV).

2 3 4 5 6 7 8 • 17 16 15 14 13

Melissa

A Father's Lessons from a Daughter's Suicide

Frank Page with Lawrence Kimbrough

Nashville, Tennessee

Dedication

My family and I would like to dedicate this book to readers who are struggling with thoughts of suicide. We pray and hope that something in this book might help you understand several things:

- That the consequences of suicide go far beyond anything you have ever imagined, affecting relationships and changing the lives of those you leave behind.
- That suicide in the life of a family often leads to the dissolution or destruction of marriages, of future plans, of dreams for many other siblings, parents, children, grandchildren, and others.
- That there is hope even when you may not feel it or understand it.
- That there are people who care for you deeply, even when the evil one has tried to convince you that you are alone, unloved, and unworthy.

We pray that you will hear a voice from the Lord throughout the pages of this book. We hope you see that God's grace is sufficient to help you in your time of deepest need. We dedicate this book to you and pray that our daughter's life and death will make a difference in your life. Remember the words of our Lord Jesus: "A thief comes only to steal and to kill and to destroy. I have come so that they may have life and have it in abundance" (John 10:10).

We dedicate this book to you, to those who choose life, to those who choose light instead of darkness, to those who choose victory over defeat.

Contents

Acknowledgments   xix

Foreword by Mike Huckabee   xxi

Introduction: From a Father's Heart   1

Chapter 1: You're Not Alone   11

Chapter 2: We All Fall Down   33

Chapter 3: This Means War   55

Chapter 4: Misconceptions   79

Chapter 5: Drugs and Depression   101

Chapter 6: The Primal Cry   123

Chapter 7: Prepare for Impact   147

Chapter 8: Back to Life   169

Epilogue: Peace   191

Appendix: A Word to Pastors   195

About the Author   201

Acknowledgments

To attempt to acknowledge help in this project is in itself a daunting task, as many have been of great assistance. I must first thank my wife, Dayle, and daughters Laura and Allison, who have walked through this journey and have been a great help in this book. These precious girls have all desired that this work—though intensely honest and sometimes very painful—would not only honor our Melissa but also help others in their dark times of life.

I also want to thank friends who have been praying and encouraging me to write this book. I cannot mention all the names, as I would not want to in any way miss anyone. However, my friends know who they are and know that they have been a great encouragement to me during this difficult process.

I want to thank prayer supporters through the many churches I have pastored and even those in which I have served as interim pastor. They have been constant in their encouragement, love, and support.

I also want to say a word of thanks to Thom Rainer, Selma Wilson, Lawrence Kimbrough, Jedidiah Coppenger, and the very capable team at B&H for devoting such passion and energy in the process of pulling this book together. It is great to work with such an encouraging team of people. My cowriter, Lawrence Kimbrough, could not have been more sensitive and more capable in this process.

Most of all, I thank my Lord for His grace, which is always sufficient. I acknowledge that this is one of the most difficult tasks I have ever embarked upon. However, it is for His glory, His honor, and to minister to His people.

Foreword

*I*t's not supposed to happen to people like the Frank Pages."
Straight from his riveting and deeply personal story of his
own daughter's suicide, this statement accurately sums up most
people's reactions to the death of his oldest daughter, Melissa.
But the truth is, such things *do* happen to the Frank Pages.
They happen to all kinds of families, of course, but suicide
can break into the lives of even godly, church-centered, Bible-
believing families. It *did* happen to the Frank Pages.

The easy thing for one of the most well-known, prominent
figures in the vast Southern Baptist Convention would be not to
discuss it at all, or to discuss it in lofty, spiritual tones that separated and isolated her act from the rest of her family. The fact
that he tells the story with a candor not often safe for someone
in such a visible position is what gives every parent and every
pastor a trip inside the darkest corridors of personal grief.

Frank is my friend, and from the time I first met him I
instantly liked him. He had recently been elected president of
the Southern Baptist Convention, and yet there was not an air
about him as one often sees in a person suddenly elevated to a
place of honor and prestige. Instead there was a quiet, refresh-
ing humility in his spirit and in his words that revealed a true

servant's heart. He was given a title, but it was only descriptive of what he did, not who he was.

When I learned of his daughter's death, my heart broke for him. I never knew Melissa. At least, I didn't meet her in life. But I do know her now. Frank's gut-level honesty about her life and her death is a powerful narrative of a father's love and a pastor's heart forced to endure the unthinkable—the death of a child by her own hand.

In all of his years of exemplary leadership in local churches and in the nation's largest evangelical denomination, he has never so effectively ministered as he does in his straightforward telling of Melissa's story. Thankfully, he doesn't try to provide sure-fire answers for all the "why" questions, and exhibits the wisdom and maturity to recognize that even if an infinite God were to reveal them, our finite minds couldn't receive them.

If you are a parent or grandparent, this book will speak to you whether or not you've had a child whose desperation led them to suicide. If you have a loved one who has committed suicide, this book will be like a candle in a dark room, warmth in a cold place, and water for a parched throat. If you are a pastor, you either have or will confront this issue in your ministry, and you hold in your hands the most useful tool I've seen to help you help those in your flock to cope.

Frank Page holds nothing back. He lays bare his soul and lets you know the depth of his own pain and grief. His openness will reach deep inside you and give you insights that are not useless sugar pills and sterile suggestions. This is life. Real stuff. It's what people actually feel and live. And God is speaking through Frank Page as never before with a message of hurt giving way to hope.

Mike Huckabee

INTRODUCTION

From a Father's Heart

I dreamed about her again last night.

Just as I do about every three or four nights.

Suddenly there she is. My little Melissa. Looking very much alive, exactly as I remember her. Talking. Laughing. Maybe fussing or fretting. Or fuming. Glad to see me. Arguing at full voice with me.

Depends on the night. I might find her either upset or upbeat. Or perhaps just *up* to something, good or bad—as likely to surprise as to absolutely exasperate. She was good at both. Ninety-eight skinny pounds on her, and she rarely gave a single one of them the afternoon off. Every ounce went into every emotion.

That was Melissa.

Yet it helps to see her. It hurts to see her. It's hard when I slowly begin to realize—whether at two in the morning or at the first gleam of daybreak—that I'm still in this room, that she's not really here, that even though she may show up in my dreams again tomorrow night or the next, her name will never again appear on my phone display, calling to ask me a question. Calling to vent another one of her wild frustrations. Calling just to call.

She always had so much to say.

Melissa.

Oh, how I miss you, Melissa.

In some ways, of course, this feeling—this vacuum, this never-relenting sense that someone's missing who should be here—is what any kind of death does to a surviving family member. I've experienced a few of those myself. Aunts and uncles. All four of my grandparents. Even my mother, who died a scant six months after Melissa did. Losses like these can certainly sting, even the ones that become somewhat expected by the time they actually occur.

But there's nothing like this. Nothing.

And if you've been there—if you've had to awaken to that first gray morning without your son or daughter being in it, snatched from your mortal presence by his or her own hand—then you know what I'm talking about. Even if the one you lost was a grandchild, a niece or nephew, a parent perhaps, a spouse, a close personal friend, we can still look each other in the eye and communicate a certain raw depth of anguish without ever speaking a word. We understand. We share something. Something horrible.

I know. I've been there.

I *am* there.

And, no, that doesn't make me an expert on all the causes, dynamics, and repercussions of suicide. I'm not pretending to be clinically trained to all the aspects involved. Even with an undergraduate degree in psychology, even with extensive theological study—PhD—even with more than thirty years' experience counseling families and individuals as a pastor, as a spiritual authority figure, I don't claim to have the perfect answer to every question. I wish I did.

But I do know what I've learned from living through this ordeal myself. I know what my wife and our other children have gone through and how hard they've endeavored, each in her own unique way, to cope with the grief and memories. More important, I know what I've seen God do, up close, right here in my own family, silently comforting us inside closets of darkness so black and suffocating I didn't realize they actually existed on earth and, if they did, how they could possibly be endured.

I'm not over Melissa's death. I admit that. I'll *never* be over it. That twenty-seventh day of November changed everything. The earth shifted under my feet. The fog rolled in and wouldn't lift. Accomplishing the simplest daily activities suddenly required dogged effort and resolve.

But I can say this: I am on my way through it, and I am still in one piece. And the *"peace* of God, which surpasses every thought"—I'm here to tell you it really can "guard your hearts and minds in Christ Jesus" (Phil. 4:7), just the way the Bible says. If I didn't know it before, I certainly know it now.

And it's with the confidence that comes from Him that I come to you in these pages, hoping I can put your particular anguish into words, hoping that in spending these few hours together as fellow travelers on this unwanted journey, you and I will both be able to look around us when we're finished and see that we've taken some big steps forward in our healing.

We can make it.

Together we can make it.

Perhaps, however, you're not a person who's reeling from the aftereffects of suicide. Not yet anyway. But if things continue as they've been going, if your child or spouse keeps interpreting life as though it's disintegrating around them, you're beginning to fear the worst. Maybe they're already threatening. Maybe they've *been* threatening for a long time, and the stress of managing their moods and emotions, trying to stay strong and positive for them against the gravitational tug of their depression, is just about to pull you under.

Believe me, I'm very sensitive to what you're feeling. In some ways you may not want to hear from a person whose daughter ultimately chose the conclusion that she did, the kind of death you're trying with all your might to avoid in someone you love. But I pray that something you read here—maybe about marital health, about handling others' judgmental opinions, about correcting biblical misconceptions, about spiritual warfare, about transforming your mind with Scripture—will not only give you counsel and comfort but also assurance that God can still change lives and work miracles. He does it all the time.

He knows where you are and understands what you're going through. God is in control. He loves you and your family. And He can do what you cannot.

Walk with me, and I'll show you.

But I'm also aware that a book of this nature is not only for people who've lost or feel like they're losing a loved one, even to such a cruel thief as suicide. You may have been attracted to this book for another reason: because you've been contemplating suicide yourself. At times, against all your better judgment, you have not been able to shake the oppressive, insistent notion that your pain has no other solution, that death is your only way out—or at least that it's preferable to going on living with these problems, with these worries, with this much guilt, with things that are this badly fractured, seemingly beyond all repair. As unthinkable as it may once have been, there are many days now when suicide is the only thing that makes any sense at all. Life is over. Life has won. You tried; you lost. What's left to really live for?

I just want you to know I'm glad you're here with me. I've been praying that you'd come. Before you make a tragic decision that you can never rethink, I want to plead with you to open your heart once more, even if just a sliver, to hear what I have to say.

I realize you may not feel like reading much. That's why I've addressed a brief letter specifically to you at the end of each chapter—to you and to others clouded with those same thoughts of despair and hopelessness you feel. If you read nothing else in this book besides those short, closing paragraphs sprinkled throughout in certain places, know that I have carefully crafted those words with you in mind. I reach out to you because I care, as do more people than you could possibly know—people who are right around you, who honestly may not realize the cavernous depths and severity of your personal suffering. If they did, they would almost certainly be there. To listen. To help. And I beg you to try rallying enough courage to tell them what's going on so they can support you with their love and sit with you in your sadness.

Know, too, if you choose to start skipping ahead and reading the book in the way I've just described, that the large number of pages you flip past—the words tumbling, tumbling by, much heavier than they seem—represent merely a fraction of the need and grief experienced by people who stand where I stand. Those pages are somewhat equivalent to the first two turns you make out of your neighborhood at the start of a thousand-mile road trip. Drops in the ocean. Gravel along the mountainside. It will take all this ink—and much, much more—to even begin to penetrate the shroud of loss, agony, and confusion left behind by some loved one who, like you, once sat alone in the dark and thought the world would be a better place without them.

Believe me, it is not.

There is not enough bold, italic type on all the printing presses in all the world to give that statement the emphasis I intend.

Even my happiest memories of Melissa make me sad. Not depressed exactly but still very bittersweet. I think of her little childlike giggle, and my heart seizes. I scissor open my birthday cards, and recognize they're always noticeably one short. I look at pictures of her and my other daughters, resting along the window ledges of my office, bundled in a thick stack of snapshots in my top desk drawer, and I start to smile, but I always feel a twinge.

And yet, just as there is hope for me, for us, for all grieving survivors to heal from this sledgehammer blow we've been dealt to the heart, there is hope for you too. I promise you. There is a better way than taking the way out. Please, I ask you, please press in here with me so we can talk about it.

Will you?

I have arranged this book around some core truths and observations that have been instrumental in getting me this far in my healing journey. Many of these things I knew already, but the shock of grief to the system has now annealed them into iron, into sheer bedrock. Others I had seen on display in people undergoing their own volcanic seasons of suffering, and now I've watched God prove them true with such personal intensity in my own life, my heart burns to share them for your good and for His glory.

The preacher in me could start listing out these principles point by point, organizing my material so it reads like a how-to manual. "Do this. Try this. Have you thought of it this way?" But the slow, steady process of healing from a wound this deep often requires (I've learned) more incubation than information. It's a journey from experience to experience, one that usually benefits from ample room for margin and rest, not a tightly scheduled tour group needing to hit all their stops for the day.

So for this reason, among others, I've chosen to interweave these various, accumulated insights with some of the most

memorable scenes from little Melissa's life: her personal struggles, her fiery spirit, the specific adversities we each endured
in seeking to shepherd and support her. I didn't think it best
to disassociate these lessons from the classroom in which we
learned them—my wife, Dayle, and my other daughters—and
I believe you'll find them easier to apply to your own heart and
situation by seeing them grounded in context.

Scripture encourages us to "comfort those who are in any
kind of affliction, through the comfort we ourselves receive
from God" (2 Cor. 1:4). That's what I hope to do. And I hope
in meeting each other here at this divinely arranged junction
point that you will be comforted and strengthened from your
stay.

I'll admit, as Melissa's father, part of my reason for writing
is simply that I want you to meet her. I don't want her to be
forgotten. She was delightful. She was difficult. I'm sure you
know what I mean, how two polar opposite traits like these
can sometimes describe the same person. But I also offer these
parts of her story in hope that you'll feel comfortable sharing
with me some memories of your own remarkable loved one as
well as the lessons *you've* learned in trying to make sense of
their all-too-short time on earth. Please make a note of this
special website (frankpage.org)—which I'll post again along
with other information at the end of the book—so that we can
keep our conversation going. I'd be blessed by that.

I invite you, finally, not to race through these pages in an
effort to reach the end but rather to sit with your thoughts and
reactions a while as you read—to savor, to receive, to assimilate.
And I pray that you'll be blessed by what you discover, by what

God speaks to your spirit as we go along, and by the way He dips His brush into the dark, crimson-tinged colors of your heart and creates as only He can a deeper shade of joy.

Frank Page
Nashville, Tennessee
Summer 2013

Consider it a great joy, my brothers, whenever you experience various trials, knowing that the testing of your faith produces endurance. But endurance must do its complete work, so that you may be mature and complete, lacking nothing.
JAMES 1:2–4

CHAPTER 1

You're Not Alone

I was in my yard-working clothes when the call came. It was Friday morning. The day after Thanksgiving. Ten more minutes and I'd likely have been out on my mower, cutting the grass in preparation for getting our house ready to sell. If so, I don't know how I would have initially heard the news. Maybe a neighbor waving panicked from her front porch, pointing first to me, then pointing to her phone receiver, back and forth, frantically motioning me over. Maybe a friend's car screeching into our driveway, engine still running, the door flying open. "Come quick! It's Melissa!"

But like you, perhaps, my first confirmation that something was tragically wrong came through a phone call. One of our church members had heard the fire trucks and ambulance wailing down their street, each of them landing in haste at Melissa's door, the emergency team bolting into the house.

I had never wanted to go here in my thinking about Melissa. Yes, she had been troubled . . . for years. Words can hardly describe what both she and we all had been through, dating back two full decades or more. But unlike the case with so many, she had never one time threatened suicide—not to my knowledge, at least—and I knew her about as well or better than anybody. So while distress and Melissa were rarely very far away from each other, the thought of her taking her own life never really seemed an imminent risk to me. Obviously it should have. We knew things had been bad, particularly lately. We were aware of some new, escalating issues. But actually we had seen her just the day before. She had been over at the house for Thanksgiving dinner. Markedly stilted and downcast, to be sure, but not . . . not anything to alert us to *this*.

How does one describe the feeling that follows that phone call? Tell me what words *you* use, when you remember? Shell-shocked? Blindsided? Stunned? Dizzy? Numb? Lost? Devastated? Physically ill?

All I know is, I had never experienced anything like it before in my life. You're simply not prepared. Fifty colliding thoughts, each attached to an immediate action/reaction, and you just begin falling forward toward your child, wherever he or she is.

And with that begins life at a whole other rung, a pain-streaked odyssey through grief, regret, and mourning and the enveloping sense that you are suddenly, strangely, savagely very alone.

I've heard many people describe the aftermath of a loved one's suicide that very way: an *aloneness*—as though we now possess, and are rapidly accumulating, a catalog of experiences that no one else can possibly understand. We're left now, bless our hearts, to duke this out for ourselves, absorbing others' well-meaning pity, the awkward responses and the only slightly less awkward silences, from people who want to know more but know they shouldn't ask. We can see their eyes dance, their thoughts calibrate, their whole demeanor involuntarily wishing to back away from us and from this uncomfortable topic. And we know that once this passing conversation is over, they can go back to their normal lives, back to their normal families, back into normal society that can never quite relate—not to us, not with this, not with *suicide*.

What a scandalously *lonely* word it is.

And yet the truth doesn't bear that out. Suicide, suicidal tendencies, suicide attempts sadly remain at rapidly increasing levels. Suicide is now somewhere between the second and third leading cause of death among ages fifteen to twenty-four—high among senior adults, high among those in late middle-age. It's recently spiking, in fact, among young women between the ages of twenty-five and thirty-nine (the same bracket as our Melissa). No one knows exactly why.

Ninety-one per day in the United States—one about every fifteen minutes or so. Take the whole globe into account, and the metric drops to one death every forty seconds, including a stunningly high percentage of people in heavily populated Asian countries like Japan and China. And for every one person who succeeds at killing himself or herself, various reporting bureaus estimate that as many as *ten to twenty-five* others have tried and (thankfully) failed.

Huge numbers. Recent statements out of the Pentagon indicate that more active-duty personnel are now dying from self-inflicted causes than are dying in combat—one suicide a day, according to the latest statistics. My friend, General Doug Carver, former chief of chaplains for the U.S. Army and now director of chaplain ministry for our denomination's North American Mission Board, confirms these troubling findings, pointing to the deep, unmet spiritual needs among those who defend our nation's freedom. Many others are coming home with such jagged emotional scars—not to mention damaged relationships, job insecurities, and financial woes—the suicide rates among military *veterans* are also reaching frightening levels. A periodical from the Department of Veteran Affairs places the number at eighteen per day, when all ages are taken into account. Add to these the individuals who are killed in high-speed, one-car crashes or from driving under the influence—auto "accidents" which are often laced with suicidal intent—and the number shoots up even higher.

Statistics, I know, are statistics. And while they represent real human lives and the heartbroken families they leave behind, we almost can't help but feel a bit distant from them, from raw percentages in newspaper print. Small comfort it gives to know that some unknown someone somewhere you'll never meet would probably be able to talk understandingly with you about what you're going through, if only they worked in your building or went to your church.

But I tell you, they do.

A young lady called me recently, a church acquaintance from years past. She said her ten-year-old son threatens to kill himself nearly every time a stressful situation crops up at home or at school. Not long ago I heard from a young teenager at a church I used to pastor whose father committed suicide after a moral failing. And it's not always the type of people you'd expect, either—the loners, the drug abusers, the heavily depressed—who choose to take their own lives. I read in the last few months about a star athlete who had signed to pitch for a major collegiate baseball program but was found dead along a country road from an apparent suicide. Another incident in the headlines recently involved a player from our city's NFL football team who failed to show up for training camp only to be located in his car in front of his former high school, dead from a self-inflicted gunshot wound.

This is not an isolated problem that happens only in certain neighborhoods or among a thin demographic of people. Suicides are not restricted to particular races, social classes, or family dynamics. The thought of it, the possibility of it, even the actual following through on it—it's virtually everywhere.

Everywhere.

I know you may feel alone, as in "left alone" with a void where this child, friend, or family member used to be. I know you may feel secluded amid a chatty, chummy, celebrity-chasing culture that doesn't want to interrupt what they're doing long enough to care about your pain or understand your need. But the pervasive specter of suicide—past, present, and future—is almost certainly on your block and under the surface. Almost everyone has endured at least a distant experience with suicide in their extended family or circle of friends, if not in their more intimate relationships.

So perhaps part of what could move you gingerly forward in dealing with your sadness and loss would be the hopefully freeing reminder that you are not as alone as you feel. There are people you pass in the grocery store aisle who share your particular brand of personal pain. There may be a driver behind you at a traffic light this afternoon who, just like you, saw something today that recalled a scene from the shortened life of his or her precious child. There is a closed bedroom door in a home not far from yours, where a solemn teenager or young adult is right now pondering his or her options as we speak.

We are not alone. We're just not.

And anytime you're feeling the loss of your loved one most acutely, anytime a haunting memory elicits an unexpected rush of sobs, anytime you're not sure you can even pry your body out of bed in the morning, those same heavy emotions are weighing down more hearts than you know, even the ones who dress them up (like most of us often do) in a crisp shirt and a brave face and go about their public business. Do not be deceived into thinking otherwise.

You are not alone.

If It Can Happen in Our Family . . .

At the time of Melissa's death, I had recently resigned as pastor of Taylors First Baptist Church near Greenville, South Carolina—a stellar congregation I had served for a little more than nine years—to accept a leadership role in one of our national SBC agencies. Average worship attendance at the church when I left was more than two thousand each week. For two years during my tenure there, I had been elected president of the Southern Baptist Convention, a nonpaid but influential position in the life of our denomination. My wife led a Sunday school class, taught piano from our home, and helped manage our exemplary life with her usual meek spirit and outstanding attention to detail. We were . . . the Frank Pages. We had a nice home in a nice neighborhood. We had friends all over the world. We had shaken hands with U.S. presidents and held the hands of countless people in our church and community who needed prayer, who needed help, who needed God.

We were not a family whose daughter kills herself.

I was a pastor, as I said, but I had decided early in life that I was committed to making my family more important than anything else. I was not going to pour myself out so completely in ministering to and meeting the needs of others that I failed to pour myself into my marriage and children. Being a husband and father was crucially important to me.

So my regular date nights with Dayle were set in stone. Sacrosanct. Nothing took the place of those unless some terrible, unforeseen emergency arose to interfere. My family was always extremely gracious and understanding toward those types of interruptions, but I did try to keep them to a minimum and not jump at every potential conflict. I drove my girls to school every morning, making sure along the way—without fail—to sing at least one rousing chorus of "You Are My Sunshine" (whether they wanted to hear it or not). There were times later on, as the churches got bigger and the demands more all consuming, that it took great effort to complete my work diligently through the day so I could be home most nights. More than once I said to some church group or standing committee, "You guys are welcome to meet every night of the week if you want, but I'm not going to be here with you." I was going home. Where I was really needed. The kids wanted to do gymnastics? We did gymnastics. The kids wanted to be in plays? We did plays. All the little girl things that little girls like to do, we did together. All of us.

We were not a family whose daughter kills herself.

Yes, Melissa—unlike our other two—was good at finding ways to get into trouble and to attract the kind of attention a young lady shouldn't want to draw to herself. People knew she was doing things that didn't square with what she was being taught at home. She invited more than a fair share of gossip toward herself and our family and left people with ample opportunities for making judgments and passing sentence.

Thankfully, humbly, I can say that the vast majority of people in the two churches I served during most of Melissa's teenage and young adult years were very supportive of her, very loving, very eager to reach out and encourage the kind of healthy lifestyle choices that came hard for her to embrace. But still, people being who they are, some couldn't hold back from making comments and whispering their opinions. On occasion I felt compelled to confront a few: "You are not allowed to talk about my daughter like that." "Please don't say those things about my family." And I'm sure when it all came down, as the news circulated about Melissa's committing suicide, plenty of them at least thought to themselves, if not to their friends, *How could that happen to somebody like the Pages?*

We were not a family whose daughter kills herself.

I'd imagine yours wasn't either.

Being made to feel unusual and categorized like that—by suicide—being convinced that others are having discussions about that, being tormented by the prospect that some are using prayer-request cover to make salacious sport of that, can leave you picturing yourself suddenly leprous and out of favor with ordinary people and families. You're enduring a circumstance that makes almost everyone else, when seen through your eyes, less flawed than you, better balanced than you, more intact than you. You're sensing the brunt (both real and imagined) of all kinds of suspicions, side talk, and stray bits of conversation.

Suicide can be a *lonely* place.

You're likely projecting onto others a good bit of that negative talk. Not all of this superiority and judgmentalism you may feel is really there. Most people are genuinely concerned and heartbroken for you, crushed at what you're going through, trying to figure out the best way to help. Their silence, those little awkward things they do that make them look embarrassed or standoffish, are not likely born from any sort of snobbery but simply from indecision about how best to approach you, even in love and compassion. The spotlight you may feel burning around your temples every time you venture into public is probably not nearly as noticeable to others as you think it is.

But when it's there, when it's real, when it seems to be pointing you out for inspection, let me tell you what I've learned about it. I've found that most people's judgmentalism—whether toward a set of parents with a rebellious child or a home that's been tainted by suicide—is a smokescreen for their own angst, for their own personal problems. When they're struggling, when they're not wanting to deal with an issue that's right in front of them, they will often focus on something or someone else to help relieve the pressure that's already on their own conscience. They'll invest time in critiquing *you* to avoid the hard work of critiquing themselves.

So here's what I want to tell you: Understand what people are like. Jesus did. He "knew what was in man," the Scripture says (John 2:25), and He knew not to take their appearances at face value. Realize that what you're hearing said (or what you're hearing is *being* said) about you and your family almost certainly has another cause. What others feel obliged to share in criticism or haughty disbelief tells as much about them as it does about you. Cold, thoughtless, priggish words give as much evidence to the nasty, carnal side of people as does any amount of poor behavior in your son or daughter, past or present.

None of us is perfect. Not a single one of us. And just because suicide has jabbed its harsh, gritty thread into the story line of our lives doesn't make anyone else more perfect than we. Nor does it make them more entitled to walk freely in the company of others without being labeled as weak or deficient, as we perhaps are now. Our lives, yours and mine, have borne a direct hit that's hard enough. We feel damaged and different *enough*. And if others make this harder than it already is by feeling entitled to observe us so analytically, then we must force our eyes open to recognize the true source behind their unkindness. And what we don't choose to confront, we must learn to let go, drawing on the character and new perspective that God is painfully growing in us through this most unsettling of circumstances.

Rather than reeling from what others think, rather than obsessing about how people are taking this, work hard to counteract the energies you could entirely exhaust in worrying about your reputation and redirect them instead into praying for those who pretend not to understand when you know good and well they're sheltering plenty of needs of their own.

I challenge you to do that.

Yet, again, our more likely challenge—it seems to me, from my experience—is found not in defending ourselves from disapproving comments but in deliberately not reading too much into facial expressions and tones of voice, not filling in words and phrases that primarily exist within our own insecure imaginations rather than other people's hearts.

Because the truth is, we are not as alone in our brokenness as we seem. And people who are being honest with themselves are aware of that, whether they admit it or not.

When I had to approach our deacons once, informing them about a situation in Melissa's life that was sure to cast an unfavorable impression on the pastor and his family, they said: "Dr. Page, we'll stand by you. We're here for you. We'll help you do whatever you need to do for your child. Don't even think about resigning." Why? Because nearly every one of those men had a child who was struggling too.

And trust me, if the greater portion of people around you were not held back by their own inhibitions, not terrified of saying the wrong thing, and not wanting to run the risk of bringing you to visible tears in public, they would almost all make clear to you that they understand, that they and their families have struggled themselves in various ways, and that you can count on them as a friend who will never judge and will only help.

You are not alone.

Do Unto Others

The same way you never expect to see a preacher's family touched by suicide, you certainly never expect to see an Old Testament prophet succumbing to depression. But that's just what we see in 1 Kings 19—Elijah, the great man of God, was first afraid and on the run from wicked Queen Jezebel and her highly enforceable death threats, then awash in his own self-pity, before ultimately turning despondent and fatalistic.

Strangely enough (or actually more common than not, knowing Satan's tactics as we do), Elijah was fresh off one of the most energizing successes of his ministry, having routed the prophets of Baal in a fiery, swashbuckling demonstration of God's just and righteous power. In addition to that, his subsequent prayer vigil in the crags of Mount Carmel had resulted in a stormy, blustery, miraculous end to three full years of drought that had charred Israel's landscape to a crisp. He must have been on a spiritual high.

Yet when depression hit, as it often can—even with God ministering personally to his physical needs, even with God gently approaching him in a "still small voice" (v. 12 KJV)—Elijah could see nothing else but the hopelessness of his condition. "I alone am left," he confessed (v. 10, then again in v. 14), believing himself to be the last of God's faithful breed, as if no one else on earth could relate to his persecuted situation.

"I *alone* am left."

Not true. God spoke of seven thousand others in Israel who had not "bowed to Baal," who had not compromised their worship and devotion (v. 18). And that's when the Lord's tone became—to our modern ears, at least, and probably to Elijah's—a bit more direct and matter-of-fact.

We'd like to see God giving him all the time he needs to recover from his dark mood. We'd like to see God patting him on the back, consoling him with "there, there" compassion. But God, knowing us better than we know ourselves, being infallibly aware of the precise moment when we've sat around in our sympathy long enough without stirring, basically said to Elijah, "All right, now, get up"—not "get over it," but "get up." And not just "Get up!" but "Go and return by the way you came" (v. 15), and get busy serving some folks who need from you what only a prophet can do for them.

One of God's cures for the loneliness of grief is the hard-fought decision to get up, get out, and get looking for ways to care for others, who—whatever their struggles and situation, suicide or otherwise—may feel every bit as alone as you do.

Very often, of course, this is the last thing we feel like doing. Yet just as often, it is the very thing we need to do. It can be what brings us out of the shadows and back into the sunlight. It's where passive resistance can be replaced by active resilience and, dare we say it—though we're exhorted by the Scriptures to "say it again" (Phil. 4:4)—it's the place where we often come the closest to *rejoicing*.

Imagine that.

I confess, the task of writing this book falls under this category of seeking to serve. It has not been an easy choice to make nor in many ways at all a pleasant task. It has brought back many hurtful memories. It's true a number of people have encouraged me to do it—to write about our family's experience with suicide and what we're still learning as a result. But even with several books to my credit and many hundreds of sermons written, I have balked more than once at writing this particular book and wondered if I could see it through to completion. I'm just being honest with you here.

But I have been truly compelled to build out this resource, hoping it will be helpful to people like you and me. And though difficult to do, hard to sift back through all the memories, God in His sustaining mercies has continually supplied what's been needed for me to craft something that's hopefully of usefulness to you and to as many others as this book will reach.

For me it's just one living example of what I'm suggesting to you: to combat whatever amount of aloneness you may feel or have wrapped yourself up in—whether from your grief over a loved one's suicide or from your shame, embarrassment, and fatigue over a child's reckless behavior—and to engage yourself in ministry and service to others.

I'm not talking about pressuring yourself to be something you're not. You may feel highly unqualified, especially right now, to have anything redemptive or worth saying to others, even in genuinely trying to comfort or encourage them. I understand that. But I'm just talking about making even the *simplest* expression of compassion, service, or generosity starting with one other person, intentionally rotating your orientation from a self-focus to an others-focus, which all by itself can be difficult to do if you've allowed yourself to withdraw and stagnate. God will fill in the opportunities if you'll look for them.

The long-suffering Job, whose story is captured in the Old Testament book that bears his name, went through the most devastating season of suffering recorded in Scripture, other than the tribulations of Jesus Himself. He lost his children, lost his vast possessions, lost his health, lost everything. But at the end of his long, torturous ordeal, including a vivid encounter with God that reformatted his entire thinking on the problems he had faced, the Bible says, "After Job had *prayed for his friends,* the LORD restored his prosperity and doubled his previous possessions" (Job 42:10, emphasis added). Scripture shows him reaching out to his neighbors, inviting them over to dinner, receiving from them sympathy and comfort "concerning all the adversity the LORD had brought on him" (v. 11) while Job likewise ministered back to them in kind.

I love that. It's not as though God's Word is saying to us that our pain and grief shouldn't matter, that we're being selfish to think of ourselves at all, that we must adopt a stoic indifference to our own needs if we're going to be pleasing to the Lord. Passages like these show us what we already know to be true but are sometimes just too afraid or defeated to actualize—that giving of ourselves gives back to us as well. Rejoining the community, both in giving and receiving, fights back against our natural loneliness.

So trust me, I am completely sympathetic toward your possible reticence to take me up on this advice. I'm aware of how sore it can make the spiritual and emotional muscles. Please don't think I'm guilting you, and please don't overdo what rightly needs to be tackled slowly. But let the counsel of Scripture guide you wisely in your steps toward and through healing. And though starting as small as you need, see where He takes you as you begin.

You are not alone.

God Help Us

During that horrible late autumn when we lost Melissa, we were in the midst of a move, as I said before, relocating from South Carolina to Atlanta. It was sure to be an odd adjustment anyway. It was the first time in more than thirty years that I was not officially in my usual role as senior pastor. Everything felt temporary and unsettled, all the way down to our makeshift housing arrangements. Here we were, trying to adjust to new work in a new city, boxes and clothes still tucked away in storage, and yet adjusting simultaneously to a world that had rocked several significant degrees off its axis.

We were in a new place in more ways than one.

And where was God?

Did you ever wonder where God was when you sat up at night asking questions that had no solvable answers? Did you ever doubt His love and goodness? Did you feel abandoned by Him? Deserted? *Alone?*

I understand if you did. I understand if you still do. Suicide is not a situation that lends itself to casual conversations with God. It hurts. And more than that, it seems as though He could have prevented it all if He'd wanted to. At those times when the loss seems the most impossible to bear, at times when you can't believe what your child is doing or has done to themselves, it can feel like God is nowhere this side of heaven to offer all that comfort His Word so confidently promises.

But I can tell you by the testimony of Scripture, He is strong enough to weather our hot accusations against Him, patient enough to withstand our desire to seek distance from Him (though such a thing is, of course, theologically impossible), and compassionate enough to feel emotion at the deep, hollow anguish that can often stand between us and our tottering faith.

Yes, we may feel He's left us all alone.

But I know that He hasn't.

And so can you.

Among my wife's first conscious thoughts upon hearing about Melissa's death (once those foggy days began to clear enough even to *contain* a conscious thought) was how much more there is to life than what we see and realize in the here and now. When a little person you once carried inside your own body and nursed at her bedside—someone you knew with the intimate closeness of a mother to her daughter—is now residing away from you in a realm you're not currently living in, it makes heaven seem more real and nearby than ever. The fact that it's not only populated by nameless saints gone before but now by one whose name we thought up ourselves, one whose crinkly nose we kissed at countless bedtimes, one whose DNA is probably still deposited somewhere within the folds or layers of our own skin . . . then I know we're not alone. *Because she's there.* She stands even now amid a "large cloud of witnesses," celebrating among the "assembly of the firstborn whose names have been written in heaven" (Heb. 12:1, 23). Yes, Melissa is there, and God is there, just as surely as He is here. And by His clock and His calendar of redemption, we are really not that far away from all being together again.

Throughout those following winter months, Dayle would often wander out into a greenway near our leased apartment in Atlanta where she would sometimes walk for an hour or more, just looking around, looking up, talking to the Lord, not allowing herself to dwell on any doubts of His love—letting her knowledge of Melissa's presence with Him draw her even closer, in fact, making her want Him more deeply than ever before. "You've got hold of her, Lord, right?" she would occasionally whisper into the morning air, feeling a tear form in her eyes, yet also a renewed sense of expectation in her spirit. God was there. With Melissa. And with us.

He's always there.

He was there in that private family room at the hospital in those first, mournful hours as I awaited word about Melissa's fatal condition, while I was also waiting for Dayle who was rushing back to Greenville after heading out of town that morning. I remember sitting there, quoting several Scriptures to myself through stinging tears, including the oh-so familiar, "Let not your heart be troubled: ye believe in God, believe also in me. In my Father's house are many mansions: if it were not so, I would have told you. I go to prepare a place for you. And if I go to prepare a place for you, I will come again, and receive you unto myself; that where I am, there ye may be also" (John 14:1–3 KJV).

Hmm. I suppose you'd expect those types of responses from a preacher and his wife. Even in a situation as dire as that. Even in the most heartrending of sorrow. But you don't need to be seminary trained or on the church payroll—or anything close to that—to experience the ever-present nearness of God. He is near to His children, even when He seems to pad by in silence without stopping to notice our breaking hearts. Our God is here. Our God is with us.

We are not alone.

> *Look: An hour is coming, and has come,*
> *when each of you will be scattered to his own home,*
> *and you will leave Me alone. Yet I am not alone,*
> *because the Father is with Me.*
> JOHN 16:32

A Letter to You

if you're contemplating suicide

I promised to pause at the end of each chapter and write a personal note to you if you're contemplating suicide or if you've entertained the idea in the past and it occasionally returns with its daring voices and deceptive suggestions. This letter is the first, and I pray it speaks to you.

I shared in this chapter about how "alone" I feel without my daughter still here, how so many parents and grandparents and spouses and friends still feel alone every day—sometimes at every hour of every day—when they think of the one they've lost.

You may feel that being "alone" would likely be a great relief to your parents or certain others with whom you share relationship, people who have perhaps complained at times that it's not your absence but your *presence* that's the problem. What they wouldn't give, you think, to make do with a little less of you . . . maybe *a lot* less of you.

But anger can cause people to say things they don't mean. And if you're in a place where you could admit that your actions or inactions could conceivably incite an angry response from someone who cares about you and is suffering alongside you, then surely you know what they really want is *you*. They are trying as hard as they can, given the history and the circumstances of this situation, and nothing would thrill them more than being back in good relationship with you.

They love you.

Even if it doesn't always come out that way.

But maybe "alone" is a good descriptor of the way *you* feel as well. And strange as it may seem for someone to say, feeling alone actually puts you in good company. I referred earlier to the Old Testament prophet Elijah, a man of deep faith and godly power, a pillar among all the personalities whose lives are recounted in the Bible. But even he endured seasons of deep depression and isolation, feeling abandoned by God and others, fretful about the future, convinced he'd lived his life for nothing. Many other great characters in Christian history have experienced the same. Many still do today.

I know that people can be ugly and mean. Hurtful.

Heartless. Discouraging to the point of cruelty. But as is often said, and is almost invariably true, "Hurting people hurt people." The ones who may have been the most unkind to you are very likely hurting somewhere deep within themselves as well. And if their rejection or resistance toward you has made you feel alone—dangerously alone, unbearably alone—I can say with nearly complete assurance that *you* are not the sole reason behind the distance they claim to want from you.

Jesus was one who was made to feel alone. "Despised and rejected by men," the Bible describes Him, "a man of suffering. . . . He was like someone people turned away from; He was despised, and we didn't value Him." Not only did He feel the angry displeasure of other people, but He was also "struck down by God, and afflicted," bearing the punishment of our sin on His shoulders, even though He (unlike any of us) had done nothing at all to deserve it (Isa. 53:3–4).

He felt alone in the garden of Gethsemane the night before His death, with no one even attempting to understand the torment and grief He was experiencing. As He was praying with such emotion that the sweat trickled down as blood from His forehead, His closest followers were nearby nodding off in sleep. "Couldn't you stay awake with Me one hour?" (Matt. 26:40).

Jesus knows. More than we can imagine, He knows.

And this One who can "sympathize with our weaknesses" now invites us to approach Him with boldness, "so that we may receive mercy and find grace to help us at the proper time" (Heb. 4:15–16)—grace for the greatest need of all in our lives (our need for salvation and forgiveness through faith in Christ), as well as grace for the everyday, the hard times, the lonely times.

You are not alone. There are people who care. There are things you can do. There are other hurting people who could benefit from your helpful presence in their lives, just as you could benefit from theirs. And above all, God cares for you and loves you deeply, and He has promised to "never leave you or forsake you. Therefore, we may boldly say: 'The Lord is my helper; I will not be afraid. What can man do to me?'" (Heb. 13:5–6).

Good question, isn't it?

And I think you know the answer.

> *Listen, LORD, and answer me, for I am poor and needy.*
> *Protect my life, for I am faithful. You are my God;*
> *save your servant who trusts in You. Be gracious to me,*
> *Lord, for I call to You all day long. Bring joy to Your*
> *servant's life, because I turn to You, Lord. For You, Lord,*
> *are kind and ready to forgive, rich in faithful love*
> *to all who call on You. LORD, hear my prayer;*
> *listen to my plea for mercy. I call on You in the*
> *day of my distress, for You will answer me.*
>
> PSALM 86:1–7

CHAPTER 2

We All Fall Down

I was born into a poor family in Robbins, North Carolina, a tiny mill town in the eastern part of the state, known for little more than being the hometown of former vice-presidential candidate John Edwards. Unable to afford a hospital stay of any duration, my parents really had no other choice but to let me make my entrance into the world from inside a local doctor's office, a nondescript little building on a typical, southern, small-town Main Street.

And from the moment I drew breath, I was a sinner in need of God's grace.

Like me, Melissa was also born in a small town—Graham, Texas—during my first pastorate: the First Baptist Church of (get ready for it) . . . Possum Kingdom Lake. Yes, I know, this part of my bio sketch almost always elicits a quick laugh from people, unless you happen to hail from near there or have kin in the area. But as the name of that little community suggests, it was not home to a lot of frills and extras—including, for example, the luxury of having an OB-GYN anywhere in town. So like every other little baby born in Graham, Texas, in the mid-1970s, Melissa was delivered by the all-purpose hands of a general practitioner.

And from the moment she drew breath, she was a sinner in need of God's grace.

The reason I mention each of our birth stories this way, punctuated by that one, ground-leveling conclusion, is because the Bible is so clear on the subject of original sin. And yet we often don't want to think it so. We don't like to deal with it—the perceived unfairness of it, the ugly ramifications of it. "Indeed, I was guilty when I was born," King David confessed in perhaps his most penitent of psalms. "I was sinful when my mother conceived me" (Ps. 51:5). Putting it another way, "There is no one who does good," he said, "not even one" (Ps. 14:3), which groups all of us within David's personal assessment of himself, the same argument the apostle Paul used in the New Testament to introduce our shared, comprehensive need for the gospel. So the Bible's teaching on human sinfulness, coupled with our real-life experience of raising children who must be taught to behave but not to be hateful, simply confirms the indisputable accuracy, really, of this living doctrine.

We are fallen. Fallen people.

Always have been. Always will be. Even with our best attempts at trying to improve ourselves.

By the time I was two or three, for example, my parents had

moved us to a much bigger, much more prosperous city. We were better off. Though I know it seems odd to say, I began sensing God's call to preach as early as age four—almost as long as I can remember—and throughout my teenage years I was already aligning my plans to prepare for the ministry. By the time I was in my early to mid-twenties, having earned my college degree with honors in three short years, then having aggressively pursued further studies toward earning a doctorate in theology, I was ready to take on my new spiritual responsibilities as a pastor with every ounce of noble intention I could muster.

And even with all of that, I was still a sinner, depending fully on God's grace.

It really doesn't matter where you're from or how faithful your family's church attendance is. Doesn't matter how many good deeds and nice accolades you can pile up. The fact remains, you and I are eaten up with sin, selfishness, and all the other necessary ingredients for making our own lives and those of the others around us miserable. And if not for the mercy of God helping us hold it all at bay, giving us the wisdom to trust Him and the courage to fight back against our own wayward tendencies, we could each end up anywhere, doing anything— even those things we swear we'd never do. That's just the truth.

The seeds of the same sins our loved one grappled with (or is currently grappling with) are also in us. The same fountain of sin that poisoned certain others enough to inflict emotionally damaging wounds on one of your sons or daughters, on a friend or family member—that very sin nature is also in us. And the same cocktail of sin and fallenness that congealed within our Melissa, as well as in your own special someone—enough that it led them to choose such a drastic measure as suicide in order to bring a stop to it—contains roots as old as the garden of Eden and as universal as every human being who's ever inhabited the earth.

This doesn't give them (or us) an excuse for what we do or what we've done. But it does point to a reason.

That's what I want to explore with you in this chapter: the fact that a person who commits suicide and a person who never comes close both share a common heritage. Part of our healing as survivors of a loved one's self-inflicted death is found in seeing them as someone who was no more fundamentally flawed than you or me or anyone else who seems to have it all so put together.

Starting from Behind

I have known a few strong-willed people in my life. One of them uses my toothbrush every morning. I don't mind admitting that I operate from a very driven, very determined, highly Type A personality. How's that for trying to put a positive spin on some inborn traits that might also be described with words like *stubborn* or *resistant*?

But of all the strong-willed people I have ever met or been around, it would take at least two or three of them strapped together to equal one of what came packaged inside our Melissa. If taking the hard way around ever presented itself as an alternative, we could almost always count on her to gravitate in that direction.

Even as a little child she would sometimes take things that didn't belong to her, then hide under the table thinking we couldn't see her. She would change the grades on her test papers and report cards so often that we routinely had to call her teachers to confirm what her real marks were. She would come down the stairs for school wearing something inappropriately revealing, and though she'd finally stomp back up to her room to change—realizing there was no getting around her mother's flat-out insistence—she'd just as likely slip the forbidden garment into her purse and then put it back on in the school bathroom before class. And sometimes she'd forget and wear the same thing home that afternoon. Or maybe she *didn't* forget. Maybe it was just her way of saying that no rules were going to force her into easy compliance.

That was Melissa from day one.

And so for these and many other reasons, we basically grounded her for *all* of her junior and senior high years. That is no exaggeration. We set up rules in the house for all of our girls, enforceable by agreed-upon consequences we'd worked out together. "If you bring home an F . . . if you talk back to your mother . . . if you're later getting home than you said you'd be" . . . then no TV, no telephone, no going out. Those were the repercussions they *chose*, we told them, by disobeying. (James Dobson would have been proud.) And so except for getting up and going to school in the morning, Melissa was largely forbidden from doing much of anything else as a result of her long list of punishable offenses. And yet even with that kind of firm, tough-love hand on her as parents, our discipline often had little to no impact on her heart, on her genuinely iron-strong will. School hours were usually all she needed for getting into a week's worth of trouble.

At the same time she could demonstrate a level of compassion and personal care for others that went far beyond the norm. One of the churches I pastored during her childhood, a congregation in Fort Worth, ran an active ministry to the deaf. Melissa suddenly, unexpectedly, became deeply interested in it. In fact, she learned sign language so capably that one night while interacting with two or three deaf friends at a girls' sleepover, they were shocked to discover later that she was actually a hearing person. That's how completely she had immersed herself in their soundless world.

On another occasion she got the idea (perhaps accurately so) that a friend of hers at school was being mistreated at home—not physically or sexually but in some manner that was apparently perceived by her young ears and imagination as abusive. So without our knowledge, and after swearing her sister Laura to secrecy, she hid the little girl in her bedroom closet for several days, sneaking food and provisions to her, blankets and pillows, letting her slip in and out through an unlocked window. I don't remember exactly how we found out she was there (a situation we quickly rectified). But those were the lengths Melissa was often willing to go in order to help a person in need.

She really did have a soft spot in her heart for the underdog, which often got her into the wrong places, like when she'd go out with certain guys that most people would probably consider "projects," not good dating material. Here was a young girl who excelled at many things—music, drama, singing, even the church Bible drill where she earned "State Perfect" status, the top level a child could achieve (despite having a broken arm at the same time, making Bible searches difficult). Her personality was funny, bubbly, and radiant—unpredictable, to be sure, but brimming with bright-eyed exuberance.

When I gave my second and final president's address at the Southern Baptist Convention, for example, she accepted my invitation to introduce me along with her sister Allison. (Laura was nearly to term with her second child at the time and not able to be there.) These formal introductions have customarily been given by the president's wife, but my sweet, quiet, reserved Dayle—though willing to do it if I insisted—asked if I'd consider an alternative. When I decided to ask the girls, Melissa jumped on it and loved every minute of it. Allison, I think, barely tolerated the whole idea, but Melissa just drank up the spotlight. What a moment that was for me!

Capability. Sympathy. Generosity. Sparkle. Yet all against a background of innate fallenness that not only tainted *her* but also taints *you*. And taints all of us. It's that Romans 7 cyclone that Paul described so famously: "I do not understand what I am doing, because I do not practice what I want to do, but I do what I hate. . . . For the desire to do what is good is with me, but there is no ability to do it. For I do not do the good that I want to do, but I practice the evil that I do not want to do" (vv. 15, 18–19).

Sound familiar? Every one of us, if we're being honest with ourselves, can completely relate to that experience, times when every notion in our right-thinking mind was pointing us true north, and yet nearly every other impulse in the rest of our body was pulling us the other way. It was as though our conscience had clasped its hands hard against each side of our face, forcibly turning our head so we were looking straight in the direction we knew we should go. But with a defiant tug away from its clutches, or an eye-rolling shrug, or a defeated sense of shameful addiction, we refuse to marry knowledge with action. We resist. We rebel.

It's what's in us.

It's what Melissa's husband, Thomas, recalls her saying to him in those final, tense, agitated moments of her life: "I just don't know why I'm like this! I feel like—like Paul said, you know—I keep doing the things I don't want to do, and I can never seem to do the things I should!"

It's what she said over lunch to my secretary, Renée, a dear friend of our family's and of Melissa's, not a month before her suicide: "Why is it so hard for me to do the right things? I see *other* people living like they should. Why is it so hard for me?"

Because from the moment she drew breath, she was a sinner in need of God's grace.

And so were we.

And so *are* we.

Whose Fault Is That?

I imagine, if we were sitting close enough to talk with each other, you'd tell me much the same story in describing the person you love—the one who finally, tragically concluded that suicide was their only escape from this vicious cycle—or who hasn't decided it yet, but in their worst moments still seems to be toying with the idea. So much good could be said about them. *So much good*. Yet at the same time there's so much turmoil, so much distrust, so much inconsistency and defiance and recklessness to go along with it. Such a closed heart. Such a misguided way of thinking. Such a weak resistance to trouble or depression. And such a strong, strong will. They were just born with it.

I hear you. Even from a distance.

And riding inside this train of thought are some of the most knotty problems that any of us ever try to get our heads around—things like: Where does evil come from? Why would God create us (and them) to endure such suffering and struggle? If He were a loving God, how could He allow this to happen? To quote from Melissa again, "Why is it so hard for me?" Why was it so hard for this person you cared about so deeply to cope with their sinful tendencies and difficulties? Tough questions. Without easy answers.

Well, let's start here: God did not create evil. God created choice. And in His creation of choice arose the possibility of evil.

I know that's a mouthful to digest, so I don't want to rush ahead without resting here for just a minute. This is something we all need to understand, as best as we can, because it's not just an abstract theological concept. It has something to do with why your loved one chose suicide. It has something to do with why you and I make the choices we still make today. It has something to do with how we react to difficult, devastating situations like these—why we sometimes say what we say and think what we think. The inborn presence of evil within us is an everyday voice and invader in our lives.

The "genesis" of this transaction, of course, comes from the experience of Adam and Eve, who were presented at the dawn of time with a flawless creation, fully provided for, free from even a

41

momentary flash of shame or guilt or failure or struggle. Their inner life was as pristine as the Eden around them, a place God Himself repeatedly described as "good" and "very good." The trees were "pleasing in appearance and good for food" (Gen. 2:9), nourished by the lush confluence of four, sparkling river sources. Pure gold and precious stones were embedded in the richly producing ground. And the man and the woman existed there in cooperative freedom with one another, pure and undisturbed by conflict, completely at peace with both themselves and their God.

"You are free to eat from any tree in the garden," the Lord had declared (v. 16). Nothing was withheld from them. Those who see a cold, dispassionate God at play in our lives would, I believe, think differently if they had been able to hover for even five minutes over the garden of Eden, a world of unimaginable delights. Free for the enjoying, free to experience without limit. And freely theirs from the Lord's gracious, generous hand. Forever, if they wanted it.

When viewed from our own vantage point—one in which our every day is unpredictably dangerous and thick with temptation, one in which our every hope comes qualified by the impending presence of death—we have a hard time picturing such perfection. That's how ideal their lives were. How very unlike ours they were.

And yet by the Creator's sovereign design, Adam and Eve were fashioned with this one complex ability: to look at God's beauty around them, feel God's pleasure within them, and still be able to choose our life over theirs if they wanted.

This choice, of course—when it came—didn't present itself

in such stark terms. The deceiving serpent was much too coy for that. He would never have mentioned the following consequences as part of his sales pitch: a new, aching sense of shame; a dimming of the entire created order; banishment from a radiant paradise; a legacy of sinful hearts to be passed down to billions more who would each receive their genetic code throughout human history.

But they *should* have known the cost. God, it must be said, had not hidden the consequences, so great was His love and desire to protect them. He didn't leave them unaware of the one crucial danger their gift of choice could invoke. He clearly warned them, "You must not eat from the tree of the knowledge of good and evil, for on the day you eat from it, you will certainly die" (v. 17). Just as we said to the girls who shared our home and lived under our rules, they were making a choice by their disobedience. For Adam and Eve that choice was a slow form of death—one that is still impacting us today.

So, no, God did not create evil, any more than we as parents casually make up consequences to dispense on our children, regardless of their behavior. But God did create choice. And through the *choice* made by that first man and woman, evil found its crease into their lives and, through them, into our own lives and into our world.

Evil is a direct result of mankind's choice not to choose God.

Before the fall, I believe Adam and Eve's health, their moods, their reactions to stimuli, even the weather patterns around them were perfect. Completely ideal, without the slightest hint of blemish. After the fall, however, everything was affected in a negative way and continues to be so until this day—from our relationships to our lines of thought to our vitamin levels to our basic motivations. Everything we see and feel and hear and experience around us is enough off-key, all the time, that our mood is usually anywhere from vaguely disappointed to heavily anxious, depending on the situation and the various factors that make us who we are. Our lives are continually being dragged down to a fallen earth, susceptible to harm and poor judgment, not because God desires it but because we have asked evil in. And it has come to stay. In all of us. We're born with it.

I was. You were.

Melissa was.

And this innate fallenness of hers affected her decisions, just as it affects yours and mine.

But that doesn't mean it was God's fault that she did what she did, any more than it's God's fault that I do what I do. The Scripture says, "Every perfect gift is from above, coming down from the Father of lights; with Him there is no variation or shadow cast by turning" (James 1:17). I simply cannot ascribe to Him anything that is evil, not based on what the Bible says, even though, yes, He allowed evil to steal something from me that was so irreplaceably precious.

I admit, I've asked myself the same questions you do: "God, why did you allow this to happen? If You're able to intervene in our world, if You hear our prayers, if You're capable of changing the direction of people's lives, why did You not change *this*? Why did you not change *her*?"

But you know what? I think He *did* intervene. Countless

times. Numerous, loving times. And yet, just as I myself have often said no to God's interventions in my life, Melissa said no to Him many times as well—over and over—*no* to His commands, *no* to His counsel, *no* to His ever-present help. He always leaves us that choice. To say *no*.

So how can I blame this most costly of decisions in her life on a lack of God's love—His love for her, for me, or for the rest of our family? No, her death was the result of life in a fallen world, colliding with both her sinful, human nature as well as the openings her sinful choices created, each of which yielded more than enough room for evil to do its work.

Does that make it fair? No.

But does that make it God's fault? No, it doesn't. No matter how tempting it is to want to place the blame there.

Good News

The only way I'd be willing to accept that God let me down by not keeping my daughter from killing herself would be this: if He had not provided her a way to deal with this fallen nature she'd inherited, if He had not cared enough to help her counteract and overcome what she couldn't even avoid in the first place.

But as many of us can attest, He didn't just *make* a way; He made His own Son the way.

He made His Son's *death* the way.

And if that's not love, I don't know what is.

Let me tell you—although I'm sure you could tell me the exact same thing—if I had been anywhere near Melissa when she was making those final choices and preparations to end her life, there is nothing I wouldn't have done to prevent it, even if it had cost me my own life. I would've considered that a suitable trade for hers. That's a father's love.

But that is nothing compared to our *heavenly* Father's love. His love for my daughter was so great that He chose, while His own Son was hanging on the cross between life and death, to restrain His all-powerful hand from initiating a rescue. That's how far *He* was willing to go to make sure Melissa's fallen nature could not ultimately consume her. Not forever. And the same love He had for her is the same love He had (and has) for your child, your spouse, your parent, your friend. For you and for me.

I ask you, how evil and cruel does *that* sound?

I am so grateful—eternally grateful—to be able to remember the night when Melissa, just nine years old, told me she realized how badly she needed God's forgiveness. I was tucking her into bed. I could tell she was wrestling with a thought that outweighed her. And somewhere within the sweet, surrendered, tearful prayer of a little girl who, even at that age, was already struggling inside with some loud, competing feelings and emotions, God reached His strong arm across the fractured, fallen relics of Eden and drew my needy daughter right to His side. She was His. As hard as her battle would turn out to be, she would always forever be His.

Because He had made a way.

Indeed, *He has made a way.*

Not long after that evening, a little friend of hers—also named Melissa—came over to the house. It was a Friday and I was home. At one point in the afternoon, she burst breathlessly through the door and said, "Daddy, I'm talking to Melissa

Jenkins outside. She wants to know about the Lord. You need to come tell her."

"Why don't *you* tell her?" I said. "Just tell her what *you* know, what *you* did."

Out she went. In she came. Again and again, always with a new question: "Daddy, can I take my Bible outside?" "Where does it talk in here about Jesus being resurrected from the dead?" "Daddy, I think she's ready to receive Christ! Don't you think you need to come out here? You're a preacher!"

"No, honey. *You* do it."

By then Dayle and I were peeking through the curtains, watching this whole encounter play itself out under the back-yard swing set. And though the window panes muffled the sound, they soon framed the precious picture of two little girls, down on their knees, hands clasped together, their eyes tightly shut, as Melissa led her little friend to the Lord, right there in the grass on a summer morning.

Yes, Melissa would have been the first to admit she didn't always live in such a way that gave evidence of the change Jesus had made in her heart. Instead of continually letting Him chip away at that strong will with which she'd come into life, she often worked hard to reinforce whatever bricks had been knocked loose during previous battles of wills. She fell on her face plenty of times before ever looking up and asking for help.

But a person's struggle against the sin in their life—even if littered with one failure after another—is often evidence that God is refusing to give up on one of His kids. "If we say, 'We have no sin,' we are deceiving ourselves," the Bible says, "and the truth is not in us" (1 John 1:8). If we don't think there's something terribly wrong inside of us, something needing a repair that we are not capable of providing by ourselves, then we are not living in reality. *But*—"if we confess our sins, He is faithful and righteous to forgive us our sins and to cleanse us from all unrighteousness" (v. 9).

As the old hymn says, His grace is "greater than all our sin."

I am well aware that you may not feel assured of your loved one's relationship with God. I say this to you with all tenderness and understanding. When I speak of our fallen nature and of God's loving readiness to free us from its clutches, you may not be able to say with confidence whether or not this person in your life ever recognized their emptiness, if they ever cried out to God in believing faith and received His sacrificial covering for their sins. One of the most crippling wounds that perhaps still today is capable of doubling you over in grief is that you may not feel completely certain your dear one is safe in heaven with God. My heart breaks with yours at the thought.

But, friend, even though it would not be biblically honest of me to deny the existence of hell and the holy judgment of God against human unbelief, we do know from Scripture that His grace is both comprehensive and immediate. The thief who died alongside Jesus on the cross cried out to Him at the full height of his pain and anguish, "Jesus, remember me when You come into Your kingdom!" to which our Lord replied, "I assure you: Today you will be with Me in paradise" (Luke 23:42–43). Neither you nor I can really know for sure whether or not your loved one threw themselves on the mercy of God at the very end. We are not the judge of such matters. But we are entitled to hope and to find comfort in knowing that the God who never stopped working in their lives knew their heart and understood their struggle.

One thing, however, is for sure: Christ's gift of forgiven sin and eternal life can be applied in your *own* heart today if you've never bowed your knee in trusting dependence on Him for your salvation and security. "If you confess with your mouth, 'Jesus is Lord,' and believe in your heart that God raised Him from the dead, you will be saved" (Rom. 10:9). Of all the things that are wrong with this world we live in, look at what our God has done to reintroduce hope into it. I pray that you have given your life to Him, to be knitted into His story line—a sure sign of better things to come.

It's Just Us

We constantly worried and struggled with Melissa. Her lying became so pervasive, she would often lie about things when the truth would've actually been more convenient for her. We eventually just couldn't believe a single word she said.

Her inability to sit still and listen at school, to pay attention to anything that didn't involve a social aspect, resulted in very poor academic performance even though she was truly a gifted child, labeled by her earliest teachers as a "genius."

By the time she started driving, the stakes of her lack of concentration grew even higher. The very first week after receiving her license, she ripped the side panel right off my car. And from there it was one ticket and accident after another. She'd be driving, drinking coffee, texting, talking, not paying attention, and just slam right into the back of people. My friend Jackie, who ran the local collision repair center, would laughingly say to her, "Well, Melissa, I don't think I've ever worked on *this* part of your car before." It was a continual battle.

But that was Melissa. That's what the people at church would say, the people at school, her friends, her sisters. They just learned to shrug their shoulders and say, "Well, . . . that's Melissa." *What're you gonna do?* I mean, sometimes, when we would feel the most helpless at keeping her in line, we'd almost want to try excusing her behavior as part of her eccentricity. We'd throw our hands up, looking around at one another across the family room, saying, "What can you do? That's just Melissa."

And yes, it was. But in more ways than any of us would like to admit, "That's just *us*" as well. Maybe we don't go around deceiving people. Maybe we've learned to steer clear of situations where our self-control is most keenly challenged and subject to compromise. Maybe we even still cannot fathom the darkened decision-making process that goes into wanting to solve one's problems by ending one's life, the way she and yours did.

But that doesn't make this person quite as different from us as we or others might be led to believe. Like us, they started from behind. That's what being born human in a fallen world entails. And if Adam and Eve hadn't done it to us, we know good and well we would've done it to ourselves.

I wish it weren't so. But it is.

I wish we didn't need God so much. But we do.

All of us.

*The gift is not like the trespass. For if by the one man's
trespass the many died, how much more have
the grace of God and the gift overflowed to the
many by the grace of the one man, Jesus Christ.*

ROMANS 5:15

— — — — —

A Letter to You

if you're contemplating suicide

I wish I knew you better. I hope one day I will. But I'm
guessing you're not often very happy with yourself. Maybe
it's because of something you've done. Or haven't done. Or
haven't been able to do. Maybe it's because of someone you
hurt. Maybe it's because others have told you for years that
you aren't worth anything—aren't pretty enough, aren't smart
enough, aren't good enough—and after a while you just start
to believe it.

It could be any of those things or one of a hundred more.

But I do know why you're dealing with them. It's because
you're broken. Not because you started out with a clean slate
and have messed it up along the way. You were broken from the
moment you were born. And so was I. So was *everybody.*

You look around and see other people, and they have what
you wish you had. They have good, healthy, easy relationships.
They have confidence. They have clean reputations. They seem
to have so few regrets or worries to keep them up at night. But
they're not as together as you might think. You know that,

don't you? Each of us woke up this morning broken. We'll drive home this afternoon broken. Needy and dependent. Whether we realize it or not.

So, yes, your brokenness is real. And hard. Overwhelming even, especially when you respond to it in ways that only end up intensifying your pain and emptiness. But you, like all the rest of us, were born with a heart, mind, and body that were incomplete, needing something else. Needing *Someone* else.

And that Someone else loves you very much.

The book of Ephesians in the Bible is actually a letter Paul wrote to a group of people who were broken and struggling. He knew they had reason to feel unwanted, unworthy, and unwelcome. He knew they may have thought they hadn't done enough—could *never* do enough—to be accepted and made clean, to have the same value as other people, to be included as part of something big and significant.

So he broke off, right in the middle of his letter, and just started praying for them. And here's what he prayed. And this is what I pray for you: "I pray that He [God] may grant you, according to the riches of His glory, to be strengthened with power in the inner man through His Spirit, and that the Messiah may dwell in your hearts through faith. I pray that you, being rooted and firmly established in love, may be able to comprehend with all the saints what is the length and width, height and depth of God's love, and to know the Messiah's love that surpasses knowledge, so you may be filled with all the fullness of God" (Eph. 3:16–19).

To feel strengthened by God's power. To be rooted and

confident in Him. To sense even a taste for the vastness of His love for you. To be filled. To be full.

I pray this for you because, even though you're broken just as I am broken, God has done something about our brokenness. He loved us enough to send His Son—our Messiah—to die in our place, to overturn our defeat, and to mend what life has seemed to damage so irreparably. We may be needy, yes, but in Christ—and Christ alone—you and I can have what we need. His love. His strength. His fullness. Go back and read of it again.

If you're not happy with yourself, then you're right, there's a reason. But there's also a reason why your life doesn't have to stay that way. Through believing on Christ, through trusting Christ, through surrendering control of your life to Christ, then this One "who is able to do above and beyond all that we ask or think according to the power that works in us" (v. 20) can heal all your brokenness and make you new and complete.

If you don't know Jesus in this way, you can. Call out to Him. "Everyone who calls on the name of the Lord will be saved" (Rom. 10:13).

And if you do know Jesus but you're still feeling your weakness and brokenness today, don't run from your source of refreshment and acceptance. Draw near and nearer. "For if, while we were enemies, we were reconciled to God through the death of His Son, then how much more, having been reconciled, will we be saved by His life!" (Rom. 5:10).

Being sinful and broken is how we came. But being cleansed and healed is how we can live.

I pray that for you today.

We were by nature children under wrath as
the others were also. But God, who is rich in mercy,
because of His great love that He had for us, made us
alive with the Messiah even though we were dead
in trespasses. You are saved by grace!
EPHESIANS 2:3–5

CHAPTER 3

This Means War

*I*f the term *mountaintop experience* derives from a single source, one of the top candidates would be a particular event in Jesus' life, "up on a high mountain" with three of His closest disciples (Mark 9:2). And like most every other mountaintop experience since then, it came with a lot to remember.

It had already been a week of intense spiritual drama and significance. After many months of responding with mouths agape at Jesus' mystery and miracles, His followers had become prone to uttering words like, "Who can this be? He commands even the winds and the waves, and they obey Him!" (Luke 8:25). But sometime during that week, the impetuous Peter had finally, formally declared what was becoming an inescapable conclusion to most of those who were closest to Jesus: "You are the Messiah, the Son of the living God!" (Matt. 16:16). They weren't just dreaming this; they were experiencing it. God was actually with them. Literally.

Jesus, however, seeing this flicker of fresh knowledge dancing in their eyes, could see something else firing within them as well. As surely as this flash of revelation filled them with awe and worship, it also triggered an involuntary reflex of pride, wondering what such proximity to God-in-the-flesh power might mean for them personally. This news legitimately signaled that the tide was about to turn for their oppressed, beleaguered people. And these Twelve were positioned on a first-name basis with the One poised to bring it about. Imagine the possibilities.

So lest they be allowed to travel too far down this heady line of thinking, Jesus immediately shocked their runaway delusions of grandeur with predictions of His own impending murder. *And* of their personal commission to take up their cross and "follow" Him (Mark 8:34). Into suffering. Into death.

It was exhilaration followed by panic.

Thoughts of victorious revenge tempered by dying struggle.

Now watch this pattern continue. By the next week they were likely still wrestling with how their nearness to the promised Messiah correlated with losing one's life "because of Me and the gospel" (v. 35). But that's about the time when three of them—Peter, James, and John—accepted Jesus' invitation to climb alone with Him up to a mountain hideaway where upon arriving "He was transformed in front of them" (Matt. 17:2), causing His face to shine like the noonday sun. "His clothes became dazzling—extremely white as no launderer on earth could whiten them" (Mark 9:3).

If this were not spectacle enough, these commonplace sons

of Hebrew heritage suddenly found themselves in the presence of two of their greatest childhood heroes from ancient history—Moses and Elijah—somehow standing there on either side of Jesus, talking with Him, as if they'd known one another for years. Then at some point during this miraculous manifestation, "a cloud appeared, overshadowing them, and a voice came from the cloud"—the voice of God Himself, saying—"This is My beloved Son; listen to Him!" (v. 7).

Again amazement. Raw power on a scale that could bend time, thwart nature, and rattle the very heavens above them with unbridled ease.

It was the mother of all mountaintop experiences.

But again, as before, lofty visions were offset by hard realities. Coming downhill from this rare, spiritual encounter, they happened upon a high-volume dispute between their fellow disciples and a pious pack of religious observers. The spark of this altercation had apparently been lit by a father's request for help. His only son had long been the victim of violent seizures, frequent enough to strip normal function from his life. Most troubling of all, these episodes appeared to spring from sinister origins—a possessing evil spirit that would cause the young man to hurl himself into the fire or plunge into deep water. His father, bereft of options, had brought him to Jesus, hoping for healing. Finding only Jesus' disciples in town, he had thought maybe *they* could help. But try as they might, they had been unable to overcome the resistance of this oppressively wicked power at work in the man's son.

What follows in the Gospel record (Matt. 17; Mark 9; Luke 9) is a vivid account of Jesus driving out the unclean spirit by the firm authority of His spoken command. A father's doubts turn to desperate belief. Shrieking and convulsing give way to breathless peace and deliverance. God's power conquers all.

But not without, for now, leaving them (and us) to continue in the struggle.

Life down here in the shadow of the mountain—though certainly an experience of hope, healing, and victory in Christ—remains one of spiritual battle. Yes, a day is approaching when like Moses and Elijah, like Peter, James, and John, we will live above the turmoil and ruckus. We who have received God's redemption through belief in His Son will escape our struggle against death and the devil and will change our permanent address to a mountaintop dwelling where joyful experiences can finally last forever.

But until then we are camped in a war zone. Not a war that can't be won but a war that must be fought.

Our precious loved ones are fallen soldiers in that battle.

And our enemy would love to see us fall as well. It brings him great joy.

On a War Footing

One thing we all know from living in this current stage of history is that the wars being fought today differ from those of past generations. For example, the conflicts of our era will almost certainly not conclude with international diplomats gathered inside an ornate drawing room or on the deck of an aircraft carrier, inking their names to cease-fire treaties. Today's wars don't end. Even in victory they just go on.

But this is not only true for armed military engagements conducted in faraway lands and reported on the evening news.

What we sometimes fail to realize, not wanting it to be the case, is that we ourselves are continually engaged in active warfare on a spiritual level—"not against flesh and blood, but against the rulers, against the authorities, against the world powers of this darkness, against the spiritual forces of evil in the heavens" (Eph. 6:12).

This is no playground we're living on.

It's a battleground.

I wrote in the last chapter about the fallen nature of man, how we are each born into a state of sinfulness and resistance toward God. This fact alone is a strike against us, right from the beginning. But in addition to that, each of us deals every day with a devoted enemy who is bent on taking full disadvantage of our weaknesses and struggles, who knows things about us we try to hide even from ourselves, who taunts us and depresses us and falsely flatters us and deceives us. Even after we've been forgiven of our sin through the blood of Christ, even with our ultimate victory secured in Him, even when like the demon-possessed man of Jesus' day we've been completely delivered from what has kept us defeated, we *still*—as long as we're attached to this earth—must contend with a foe who wants to steal every ounce of life and freedom from us that he possibly can.

So for you and me, this means we're not only dealing with our grief, as heavy and painful as it can often be. We also have a real-live enemy out there, seeking to burden our deep sense of sadness with the added weight of anger and hatred and doubt and disillusionment. He wants to turn this normal emotional response of grief inward on us, shaming us, deadening us, pummeling us until all we want to do is check out on life.

That's what makes it a spiritual war.

We aren't just dealing with noticeable areas of strain in our marriage and family. We're also dealing with an evil opponent who knows that today's loss of temper and patience can become tomorrow's separation and divorce. He knows precisely which words and phrases are most effective at keeping that pot of blame and resentment stirring, causing us to forfeit whatever amount of healthy ground we've retaken in our relationships, further distancing us from the ones we love the most.

It's spiritual, see. And it's war.

It means we're not just haunted by disturbing dreams, or lethargic from a lack of physical energy, or easily agitated by minor inconveniences and disturbances. We are also being watched and monitored by a spiritual entity who can turn any of these experiences—and hundreds of others—into opportunities to destroy us. He wants us convinced that the severity of our loss gives us an excuse for reverting to any pain remedy we choose, while he leaves us thoroughly *unconvinced* that these same sources of temporary relief will only succeed at keeping our wounds open and bleeding.

As bad as our situation is, as traumatic as suicide always is, there is a way to make it worse. And our enemy just lives for that. It's his specialty. *Spiritual warfare.*

We would like to think that this wicked reality is not so. Most of us feel much more comfortable believing that we are only opposed by things we can see and quantify and choose to combat in our own logical, five-senses way. But what I'm saying—what the *Bible* is saying—is that much of what presses against us as we try to heal from this suicide in our lives, or as we try to extinguish the volatility in a disturbed child or spouse's life, is actually being orchestrated in realms beyond our imagining. And in order to try counteracting it, we need more than good friends and gritted teeth. We need spiritual power. Spiritual defenses. Spiritual tactics.

We need God.

The one, true, living God, who alone is able to overcome *through* us the torrents that sweep *over* us—the one who sent His Son that we "may have life and have it in abundance" (John 10:10).

A Battle against Abundant Life

This passage I've just quoted from John 10 ends up telling us a lot about Jesus, as well as a lot about our enemy, and a lot about us. This is the place in the Bible where we are introduced to Jesus as "the good shepherd" (vv. 11, 14). He says He is not like a "hired man" (v. 12) who doesn't care about the sheep, who's not personally invested in their safety and welfare, who in the event of a predatory attack is more likely to run away to save his own skin than to attempt a protective rescue.

The Good Shepherd *knows* His sheep. And His sheep know Him. They know His voice. They recognize when He is near. They trust His loyalty to them. And even if the sheep are too blind or dumb to completely understand His intentions, He shows His great love for them by boldly proclaiming, "I lay down My life for the sheep" (v. 15).

Standing where we stand, of course, on this side of the cross, we know the Good Shepherd has made good on that promise. In fact, He has ascribed to *goodness* a new definition—the ultimate definition, a sacrificial definition. For you and for me.

But the *enemy* of the sheep could not be more different from the Good Shepherd. He is instead a "thief and a robber" (v. 1) who has climbed into the sheep pen through "some other way"—like through this tragedy of suicide in our lives, for example. He is "a stranger" in our midst (v. 5) who has found a point of entry into our hearts, minds, and emotions. But his "voice" does not have the same familiar, comforting ring as the Shepherd's. The enemy's voice would lead us astray if we followed it. He would lead us to destruction.

That's because this thief, the Bible says, "comes only to steal and to kill and to destroy" (v. 10). Those are his deadly aims for us. Job number one to him would be to keep us eternally lost and separated from Christ. That is his ultimate mission. But if he's too late or if he's left himself too exposed to prevent us from being drawn in by the Savior's love, from being forgiven by His grace, from being rewarded through Christ's merit with a prepared home awaiting us in heaven, then don't think for a moment this spiritual prowler will accept being spurned so easily—because second on his list of acceptable objectives is the goal of stealing what's left from believers like you and me. Rendering us weak. Defeated. Stunted. Hollow. Thin. Anemic.

That may be the best he can do at this point, but he is very good at doing it.

So if you're a Christian attempting to cope with a loved one's suicide (or attempting to respond to their suicidal threats and intentions), do not be surprised to feel yourself being motioned away from God, questioning biblical promises you always knew to be true, avoiding the church and its people, abandoning spiritual practices that used to be normal habit for you but now seem so . . . unnecessary, unhelpful, almost painful and upsetting, counterproductive.

I'm telling you, you're not just tracking this way because you're tired and in a weakened state, not just because you're sad and lonely, feeling incapable or inferior. No, *forces are fighting against you.* You have been targeted by "rulers" and "authorities, by "powers of . . . darkness," by "spiritual forces of evil in the heavens" (Eph. 6:12). This is an all-out war against you and your abundant life in Christ. Get used to it.

But as soon as you're clear on that, become clear on this: the enemy's freedom and motivation to come against you does not give him *carte blanche* to rob whatever he wants from you. You can resist him. You can stand your spiritual ground. You can hold on and even advance against the onslaught of this attack.

And here are three proven reasons why this is true:

1. We have weapons. Though we live in mortal bodies that are limited by our own muscular and mental strength, "the weapons of our warfare are not worldly." They are not limited to our best personal efforts but are "powerful through God for the demolition of strongholds"—such as the rejection of unbiblical thoughts and beliefs in our minds, the exposure of any unhealthy habit patterns we're pursuing. And by trusting in Christ and immersing ourselves in His Word, we are able to wrap our fists around these potent battle weapons, able to "demolish arguments and every high-minded thing that is raised up against the knowledge of God, taking every thought captive to obey Christ" (2 Cor. 10:4–5).

2. *We have armor.* Empowered to go on the offensive, we are also prepared to defend ourselves against whatever our enemy would hurl against us. We stand here today "with truth like a belt around your waist, righteousness like armor on your chest." Our feet are "sandaled with readiness" by the "gospel of peace"—a living truth that is able to soothe our fears, our doubts, and our insecurities. The "shield of faith" knocks away "all the flaming arrows of the evil one." The "helmet of salvation" protects our spiritual senses from being confused and misinformed, while the "sword of the Spirit, which is God's word" covers any other vulnerable spot with its deflective strength. Prayer, too, keeps us "alert" and awake "with all perseverance," always watchful and discerning, even when our own reserves feel so woefully inadequate (Eph. 6:14–18). We have weapons. We have armor. And what's more . . .

3. *We have the enemy's playbook.* As human beings, we are susceptible to being hurt in many areas—physically, emotionally, financially, relationally. And yet Satan knows the only place he can really influence us and bring us down is by infiltrating our minds. That is where the X is marked on his battle plans, where his laser beam is pointed. And this is why God instructs us (and enables us) not to be "conformed to this age, but be transformed by the renewing of your mind, so that you may discern what is the good, pleasing, and perfect will of God" (Rom. 12:2). In order to win the spiritual battles, we must force our thoughts to dwell on and believe what the Scriptures teach us, even when our feelings, instincts, and observations are leading

us to believe something else. If we can win against him here—
in the mind, in our control center—we make it immeasurably
harder for the enemy to execute any of the other maneuvers he's
drawn up against us.

We make it hard for him to run off with our abundant life.

Spiritual Signs

OK, I know we've covered a lot of biblical territory in
this chapter, and granted, it's not the easiest concept to grasp.
Spiritual warfare. The whole idea is so cosmic sounding, I
understand why it doesn't immediately seem to relate very
closely with what you're up against, when all you know is that
you're hurting and sore. You probably came to this book simply
in hopes of finding something to take the pain away, to hear a
word of encouragement and peace, to help you make sense of
what's happened, of what's happening.

But spiritual warfare *is* what's happening. It's as real as our
weekly calendars and our list of weekend errands. It's as current
as the headlines in the morning paper and the decimal points in
our checkbooks. Just because we're more accustomed to thinking in black-and-white terms and in three standard dimensions,
that doesn't mean we're not subject to satanic notice and attack
as a matter of ongoing routine.

After all, doesn't it explain some things? Where do all those
painful mental images come from, arriving without notice,
often at our most fragile, vulnerable moments? Who is the
source behind the incessant "what ifs" that taunt us with their
unanswerable questions to unalterable life events? What else
would inspire us to turn against someone in seething, harbored

anger, as if the sting of our heated rebuke could achieve anything else besides adding to their personal sense of guilt, pain, regret, and loss?

Does this sound like the work of our heavenly Father, who knows "how to give good gifts to [his] children" (Matt. 7:11), who the Bible says would never respond to our request for bread by giving us a stone or to our need for nourishment by handing us poison? Don't these tactics sound a lot more like the one who was "a murderer from the beginning," "the father of liars" (John 8:44), "a roaring lion, looking for anyone he can devour" (1 Pet. 5:8)?

Exactly. That's what I think too.

So even though we may not possess the capacity to understand the spiritual realm completely, we do know enough to ascertain that the whispers of hell only sound enticing for all the wrong reasons—like revenge, temporary relief, rejection of discipline, refusal to deal with reality.

The spiritual nature of Satan's attacks would certainly explain the fingerprints we saw on Melissa's life throughout her high school, college, and young adult years. Even though she believed in Christ as a child, the alluring voice of the enemy could so easily tease her with the thrills of peer acceptance, with self-destructive habits that only resulted in demeaning her sense of worth.

Occasionally the enemy would overplay his hand, like the time Melissa was caught with several other kids who had gone off-campus for some kind of inappropriate escapade, only to be hauled before the entire student body at her Christian high school to publicly repent of their acts. You'd think a jolt like this might have served to grab her attention, opening her eyes to what she was losing by abandoning her right to abundant life. And yet she largely seemed oblivious to the spiritual warfare that was so obvious to the rest of us, all the while letting the enemy succeed at his dirty work—creating a steady buildup of guilt and treacherous habits that etched their scarring grooves onto her heart and onto the direction her future would take.

The devil's inroads eventually expanded to so many lanes that by the time she got to college, finally out from under our roof and restrictions, his voice was just about the only one to which she responded anymore. She rarely went to class. She did whatever felt good and figured she would worry about the consequences later. She drank and danced and partied, anything to keep her from feeling bad about what she was doing.

Oh, how we tried fighting the battle *for* her and *with* her. How we prayed and prodded, flinging ourselves between her and her enemy. Not that we were perfect, but we were persistent. Dayle, in fact—in an uncharacteristic move for a woman so quiet and peace loving—even set off one late afternoon to drive the hour and a half to Melissa's school and packed up her things to bring her home, right there in front of her friends and roommates.

But we continued to endure such horrible confrontations with her, after which she'd sometimes storm out of the house and be gone for days, not telling us where she was. Eventually she'd come back, but the lies she'd been taught to craft and create by that "father of liars" left us with no way to trust her or to manage her behavior without keeping our other daughters nervous and on edge. This battle for her heart, her soul, her love—her life—continued to rage on, on every front, year after year.

But perhaps, though she rarely if ever let us see it, she recognized more of what she was dealing with than she was willing to admit. Years later, in a moment of unusual clarity and transparency, bravely sharing her public testimony with a women's conference audience, she looked back on that night when her mother snatched her out of her dorm room and said, "I will never forget how embarrassed I was in front of my college friends, but at the same time I felt so relieved and rescued. I remember praying during the ride home, just thanking Him for rescuing me." She would say of that season in her life, "I could hear the Holy Spirit inside me, just begging me to stop and let go." Even in those moments when she was being held so firmly captive by the enemy, she knew her God had not forsaken her. "But the things of the world," she said, "were right there in my face, calling my name, and I continued to give in."

There it is. The battle. She did feel it. We all feel it. And even when we don't, it's still there just the same. Tugging at us. Tempting us to give up and quit if not to rebel. Tearing away at hearts already so broken and shattered, our gut response is often just to give in and let him have his way. It hurts too much to try resisting. *Who cares anymore?*

Well, I do.

I care for you, just as I care for my family, just as I care that my own life, though now bearing this nasty scar of suicide, still represents accurately the healing grace and power of my Lord and Savior. I care enough to risk sounding hyper-spiritual in order to remind both you and myself that what the Bible says about our life experience on earth is true whether we perceive it that way or not.

We're in a battle against a spiritual enemy—a battle for our minds, our sanity, and our future.

And for that we need a battle plan.

Seven Steps to Spiritual Victory

As one who knows, like you, how hard it can be to stay focused each day not only with these giant, oppressive memories occupying our minds but also with a sworn enemy eager to turn them against us at any moment, we need spiritual strategies for fighting back. As Paul said, "Though we live in the body, we do not wage war in an unspiritual way" (2 Cor. 10:3). That's because the ordinary methods of fighting don't work against this enemy. He doesn't wince at our resolutions and improvement plans. But I have found these following tactics to be successful in helping me appropriate God's power and resist the pressure to ball up and sink to the bottom.

1. Identify the source. Like I said, Satan's main point of entry for spiritual attack is the mind. And this is why being "transformed by the renewing of your mind" is so important (Rom. 12:2). You must keep your senses trained to the presence of new or repeat thought patterns, not allowing them eight-lane freedom to run up and down inside your head without being pulled over for closer inspection. Staying renewed in mind means keeping the floodlights on and the alarm systems triggered, ever on the watch for intruders into your mental living space.

When you become aware of a thought, inclination, or emotion that registers in your active thinking, perhaps while you're driving home from work or lying awake in the night, intentionally stop and ask yourself where this idea is likely coming from.

Sometimes locating the source is easy and evident. Some thoughts are so obviously wrong, you just know they need to be dismissed, even if they give you a rising sense of control or relief. But sometimes you're left feeling confused: *Is that true? Am I right to feel this way? Should I really consider doing that? Would I be wrong to say those words?*

John 14:17 tells us the Holy Spirit is the "Spirit of truth," that He "remains with you and will be in you." So for a believer in Christ, His Spirit is an active, onboard guide to help you navigate these often difficult judgment calls and fact-finding missions.

No, asking Him to help you discern the source of a given thought is not like putting a quarter in a slot. Much of it involves developing a relationship with Him, the kind that continually helps you recognize His voice above your own and above your enemy's, the way Jesus said the sheep recognize the voice of the Good Shepherd. But the Spirit is gentle and can be trusted to lead you rightly as you surrender your will to His control. It's a growing process, a maturity process. But the more you make this a regular exercise, the wiser your thinking will become. You'll say, "My Lord would never encourage me in that direction," or, "He wouldn't shame me like that over matters I've already confessed and He has forgiven." Find out where those thoughts are coming from. "For God has not given us a spirit of fearfulness, but one of power, love, and sound judgment" (2 Tim. 1:7).

2. Take every thought to its logical conclusion. One way to help you identify the source of a stray thought is to ask yourself where it would take you if you followed it all the way home. If you were to act on it or be governed by it, would it enhance your healing, or would it more likely hinder your growth and recovery? Would it draw you closer to God? Would it make you a better person, parent, spouse, or friend? Would it encourage and inspire others if you expressed it, or would it probably only dishonor your God or make Him look unable to lead His children through hard times with grace, strength, and perspective?

Your and my hope, even as suicide survivors, is that the "words of my mouth and the meditation of my heart be acceptable to You, LORD, my rock and my Redeemer" (Ps. 19:14), that we will "know the truth," and that the "truth will set [us] free" (John 8:32). By putting our thoughts through the paces of careful, spiritual scrutiny, we repel an enemy whose success depends on our being lazy about vetting his sneaky suggestions and insinuations.

3. Confess any thought you've wrongfully accepted. As the Lord convicts you of embracing unhealthy, unwholesome thoughts—perhaps against Him, perhaps against others, perhaps against the loved one whose suicide has rained such torment on your soul—be quick to release those harmful notions and admit you've been deceived. God is quick to forgive you and eager to set you on a course of well-being and usefulness. As I've mentioned before, "If we confess our sins, He is faithful and righteous to forgive us our sins" (1 John 1:9). That is His promise. That is His nature.

So remind yourself that you belong to Him. Remind yourself that He understands what could make you feel this way or want to respond like that. And remind yourself that your enemy is the one who wants to see you continue in either ongoing error or in the shameful rut of feeling unforgiven, as if God's anger will never be satisfied against you. *Not so.* Keep coming back. Keep inviting His cleansing. Keep accepting His truth as your only ticket forward.

4. Develop good habits. Suicide can rock us so violently, opening us up to such heavy spiritual assault that we can easily give in to the temptation of becoming passive and unassertive. Curling up. Vegging out. Signing off. And while active rest and healthy diversions can all naturally contribute to the healing of blunt trauma, can't you also see how our caving to lazy inactivity and sloppy discipline only makes us easier pickings for Satan's destructive deceptions?

You need quiet time with God in His Word and in prayer. You need the structure of a regular schedule and realistic goals to achieve. You need the accountability of trusted Christian friends who have reason to care for you but also permission to speak plainly with you. You need limits on such empty-calorie consumables as television and mindless entertainment. You need the steady rhythm of church and active engagement in its life on a personal, local level. And you need to guard these various pursuits so zealously that the enemy has little room for inserting idle thoughts into your inactive brain. "Whatever is true, whatever is honorable, whatever is just, whatever is pure, whatever is lovely, whatever is commendable—if there is any moral excellence and if there is any praise—dwell on these things" (Phil. 4:8).

5. Position your armor daily. We've already talked about the spiritual armor God has given us to help defend ourselves against spiritual attack. But lest these battle implements sound like mere biblical imagery, I encourage you to go through the mental exercise each morning of placing these actual defenses into position: the belt of God's eternal truth, the breastplate of His righteousness applied to your heart, shoes for taking His gospel message with you into each day, the shield of faith, the helmet of His promised and hard-won salvation, and the sword of His unshakable Word.

If you start to feel your armor sliding off by mid-afternoon, check again to be sure each piece is locked into battle readiness. And before you face the long, often sleepless hours of the night, clamp them back on as a guard against Satan's sneak attacks under cover of darkness.

The armor is not a kid's toy set or a game for superstitious believers. It is an assemblage of spiritual might in Christ Jesus. Strap it on and see for yourself.

6. *Practice godly common sense.* Not every area of spiritual victory comes from doing things that are stereotypically Christian. Some of your ability to prevent additional losses and thievery will spring from strategies that are simply smart and make good sense.

Examples of these might include: (1) not jumping into activities outside your gifting or skill set, things that are likely to drain you emotionally or frustrate you with unnecessary complications and failures; (2) making sure you stop to recharge your batteries instead of overextending yourself in an attempt to keep your mind occupied; and (3) limiting your exposure to emotionally draining people whose negativity or neediness can threaten what God is doing to help you recover.

Be free and honest enough to know what helps and what hurts you. And if you're not sure you're implementing the best principles, ask someone you trust to share with you their wise opinions.

7. *Write down your victories.* *We* remember our defeats; we forget our victories. Satan never stops reminding us of the former; he never stops to mention the latter. So I challenge you to start, if you haven't already, keeping a daily, candid journal of what's going on in your life. It won't all be pretty, not for people like us who've been through the losses we've endured. But you will be surprised, if you're faithful to log even the smallest hurdles and milestones, how often the evidence of God's helping hand has reached out to steady and support you.

Return to your journal often to read and reread it. Create this tangible way of recalling the slow, gradual gains of progress He has brought about. Every lesson is an investment in the next one. Every blessing opens the door for receiving another. And every spiritual victory builds your confidence that God can defeat whatever is knocking on your front door today.

Spiritual warfare. It is what confused, weakened, and stole life from our Melissa. And it is what badgers each of us today, whether we're caught in the active grind of relational difficulty with a family member or in the ashes of their senseless death. It is an ever-present reality even for those who think they can regain their strength if they just knuckle down and deal with things in a levelheaded manner, one at a time.

No, they can't. We are spiritual beings encased in a physical world. And that part of our natures which will one day soar to be with Christ is the part our enemy is savoring to deaden and demoralize. "Be strong in the Lord, and in the power of his might" (Eph. 6:10 KJV), and you will claim increasing victories you thought had been stolen from you forever.

> *God, hear my cry; pay attention to my prayer.*
> *I call to You from the ends of the earth when my*
> *heart is without strength. Lead me to a rock that*
> *is high above me, for You have been a refuge for me,*
> *a strong tower in the face of the enemy.*
> PSALM 61:1–3

A Letter to You
if you're contemplating suicide

If I asked you to tell me the main issues and problems that are giving you little reason to live anymore, I know you could name them one by one for however long we were able to talk. And I know that each of them—or at least the accumulated weight of them—feels so gigantic and monstrous, so overwhelming, that you often cannot see yourself surviving them or making it safely around to the other side of them.

And while, yes, I agree with you that these matters are legitimate and serious, you need to know there's a spiritual enemy at work against you whose job is to make them seem more enormous and insurmountable to you than they actually are.

He is trying to kill you. Do you see that?

The Bible, in a verse I quoted earlier in the chapter, calls this enemy a "thief"—one who "comes only to steal and to kill and to destroy" (John 10:10). Death is his goal for you. He knows the damage it can do not only to you but to your family, to your friends, to your church, to your testimony and ministry as a Christian. If he can destroy you, he can destroy a generation. If he can steal life from you, he can steal peace and joy from five, ten, twenty others who love you and care about you, who will be left to deal with their guilt, their pain, their hurt, their loss, their grief, their sadness, their struggle.

If he can cause you to see death as a viable option—even contorting your thinking enough to view it as almost a noble, heroic act, something that will give others relief from having to deal with you and your difficulties—then he can leave a mark on others that will never go away.

These suicidal thoughts often feel like they're starting with you, as if you're coming to this conclusion on your own. But Satan is the encourager, the motivator, the impetus behind every destructive, violent, fatal thought that passes through your mind. And he's banking on the high probability that you'll catch them and pull them in and claim them as yours.

So I'm asking you to do something different with those thoughts. The Bible tells us we are not hopeless slaves to what others tell us or how they describe us, that we have been granted God's authority and backbone to take "every thought captive" and force it to be analyzed by what His Word says is true (2 Cor. 10:5).

You may or may not have a great familiarity with the Scripture, and so you may not always have anything other than your God-given sense of right and wrong or your common sense to help you know how to sort out what's true or not. But

I want you to consider doing this one thing for me—it's all I ask: say and repeat the following verse until you hopefully have it memorized, always on hand to help you recognize the grand extreme between what Satan wants of you and what the Lord Jesus wants *for* you.

John 10:10, the words of Christ—"A thief comes only to steal and to kill and to destroy. I have come so that they may have life and have it in abundance."

Life.

As hard as yours can be sometimes, perhaps seemingly *all* the time, Jesus has an "abundance" of life for you that is stronger than even the iron grip of death, and you know how strong that can be! His love for you, His *life* for you, is more consuming than Satan's hatred of you and his desire to deceive and destroy you.

Yes, to be able to experience this life will involve some repentance. Some forgiveness. Some attempts to make things right that others may spurn if they don't believe you and aren't ready to go there with you. But the Lord Jesus will go there with you, even when the healing and the recovery are hard and slow. His voice will be the one that is ever drawing you toward life, toward hope, toward rescue, toward authentic freedom.

"Some wandered in the desolate wilderness," the Bible says, speaking of people in past generations who once felt the way you perhaps feel today. "They were hungry and thirsty; their spirits failed within them. Then they cried out to the LORD in their trouble; He rescued them from their distress. He led them by the right path to go to a city where they could live" (Ps. 107:4–7).

Where they could . . . *live.*

Your enemy doesn't want you to know about that "city." But it does exist. Right here on earth—wherever a person like you stares a deathly thought in the eye and says they're choosing life, no matter the cost.

I believe that man or woman can be you.

This is why you must take up the full armor of God, so that you may be able to resist in the evil day, and having prepared everything, to take your stand.
EPHESIANS 6:13

CHAPTER 4

Misconceptions

*M*elissa needed people. Needed attention from people. Needed fun. Needed activity. Needed to be in control of others. Needed her way. Needed autonomy. Melissa . . . needed.

So when she returned from her abbreviated, two-month tenure as a college student, what she *needed* most, she thought, were places to go where she wouldn't be asked what she was doing back home, people who would just accept her story—whichever version she wanted to tell—and would give her the kind of camaraderie that fed into her hunger for acceptance and companionship.

And she found all of this through going to AA meetings.

Now I'm not knocking Alcoholics Anonymous or any other such organization. I believe these groups can be a helpful source of recovery and accountability, a vital tool in helping people overcome their addictions. But Melissa was not an alcoholic—*she* knew it, *we* knew it. The things she did, she did for her own flawed reasons, and though alcohol was sometimes in the middle of it, she could just as easily meet her needs without it. Yet at the invitation of another person who wanted to help, Melissa began attending AA meetings on a fairly regular basis, knowing full well (she later admitted) that she was simply using it to give herself an acceptable excuse for her erratic behavior.

What she found, though, was her drug of choice: *attention*. She was the cute little blonde in a circle of people mostly fifty and over, who treated her with the doting affection they might give a daughter or granddaughter. Even those participants who were closer to her in age typically wore their hard experience on their faces and complexion and overall demeanor, leaving her as the bright, charming star of every get-together.

So it wasn't long before she'd attracted the kind of attention a young single woman enjoys from other men, in particular from a fellow AA member who made her feel special in his company. They started to see each other on the side and had only been dating a few months when he relapsed into his former pattern of drug abuse, causing their relationship to fall shakily apart.

But not before Melissa found herself pregnant with his child.

If you've been in her shoes, you know the numbing mixture of fear, worry, and panic that grips you, slowly at first, then like a freight train as your knowing suspicions are officially confirmed. If you've been in our shoes as parents, then you can relate to what we initially felt: the devastation and disturbing anger. Even with all the troubling issues we'd faced with

Melissa up to that point, pregnancy introduced a level of lingering, disorienting weight that was heavier than anything we'd experienced before. Every other discovery of troubling behavior, though naturally upsetting, had always left open the option of being correctable if we could only get through to her. This one, however . . . pregnancy . . . this one wasn't going away.

But in addition to expected reactions like these, we were also forced to deal with another, which somehow proved more bewildering than all the rest.

Melissa, instead of coming to us first, had confessed her situation to a friend, a dear lady who called and asked if we'd please come over, that Melissa was there and had something to tell us. After we'd hurriedly arrived, the two of them partnered to break the news. But almost as soon as this revelation of hers had shattered like broken glass at our feet, Melissa hopped up unexpectedly and said, "OK, well, I've told you now, so . . . how about we go get some Mexican food?"

Uh—

What?!

Dayle and I stared blankly at each other through tear-moistened eyes, the shock still registering on our faces. *She wants us to go out for dinner at a time like this? Does she not feel the same thing we're feeling? I don't care if I ever eat another bite in my whole life!*

But this emotional immaturity, though I believe never more shocking to us than on that day, had really been evident for many years. Our other two daughters, each younger than Melissa, had progressively struggled with her as they grew and developed and basically surpassed Melissa's level of self-awareness and emotional health. Her hunger for attention had become a source of embarrassment and irritation that continually rankled their relationship as siblings, a disconnect Melissa could never seem to identify as originating in herself.

In this case, however, sitting there in shock and shame in a strange living room, all we could do was sit back and wonder when if ever she was going to find herself. What would we need to do now to help her through this new ordeal? Where was this whole thing taking us? How would it end?

If we had actually known the answer, I don't know *what* we would've thought.

Strike Two

There's more to tell, of course, about this turn of events, and I'll be able to tell some of it later. But for the purpose of this chapter, I need to fast-forward to another significant occurrence in Melissa's life that held a great bearing on her future.

She became engaged to a young man who seemed to make her happy, which made us happy as well. She planned her wedding. Did all the bridal things. But inside she started to realize that she was pushing marriage too fast, that the void she felt for a man in her life was more of a motivator than this particular man himself. Two months before the ceremony was set to take place, she abruptly broke off their engagement.

The intervening years were filled with ups and downs. She worked hard to pay back the college tuition she had wasted. We kept a little schedule on the refrigerator, and she methodically chipped away at it until she'd refunded us every dime. She was proud of that. So was I.

Our family's move from Augusta, Georgia, to Greenville, South Carolina, proved a healthy transition for Melissa, a fresh start she desperately needed, and she knew it. One autumn night a couple of years after our relocation there—having received such accepting love from our new congregation, having enjoyed a period of life filled with quite a bit more steadiness and consistency—she experienced a memorable moment with the Lord where she realized in plain terms how much damage her sin had caused, how many people she'd hurt, how desperate she'd become for change, and how much she loved Him and wanted to live for Him. It led to a time of spiritual and physical rest that yielded as much fresh air in her life (and in our lives) as we'd had in . . . I don't know how long. Forever, it seemed.

Not long afterward, God led her to Thomas, a guy she met through the singles ministry of our church and who pleased us so much with his new commitment to Christ. How interesting for Dayle and me to meet and get to know a man for whom we had been praying since the day Melissa was born—not by name, of course, but by asking the Lord to bring a godly young man into her life one day to be her husband, just as we had done for all of our girls. They went to Bible studies together, prayed together, encouraged each other in their lives as believers, and genuinely fell in love. In November 2005, a year and a half after they'd first met, they were married in a beautiful ceremony at our church.

It was so good to watch. So, so good. To see her growing and getting her feet up under her. We really thought, as we hoped and prayed, that her hardest days were behind her.

Until cancer.

Melissa had a proclivity for being a hypochondriac. Self-professed. She was always extra sensitive to things that were happening inside her body. So unsurprisingly, she was quick to notice—about the time she and Thomas were married—that some small knots had developed on one side of her neck. The ENT doctor she visited didn't initially see much to be concerned about, but after a year had passed and the knots had become a bit larger and sore to the touch, he scheduled her for a CT scan, followed by a PET scan, followed by a biopsy, followed by an official diagnosis: Hodgkin's lymphoma.

Her prognosis was fairly good and positive, even though the cancer had not been caught particularly early. Hodgkin's, you may know, is traditionally much more treatable than its near cousin, *non*-Hodgkin's, which tends to be more aggressive and fatal. But still, six grueling months of chemotherapy, even with a hopeful outlook at the other end, is daunting to the most stalwart of individuals. For Melissa? Oh, dear. We were worried sick about how she would react to this medical regimen. We feared it could easily send her back to an emotionally fragile state she had fought so hard to leave.

Dayle, bless her heart, took wonderful care of Melissa. Along with Allison, they *both* took wonderful care of her. Allison even decorated her home for Christmas, a task she excels at. All the family attempted to be by Melissa's side during each cancer treatment. Even though my personal schedule was hectic, having only recently been elected to my first term as president of the Southern Baptist Convention, I was able to attend many of her treatment sessions.

On all the other mornings when they weren't at the

treatment center, Dayle would drive over to Melissa's as Thomas was leaving for work and would bring her back to our house to spend the balance of the day. Dear members of our church brought in meals three days a week—Monday, Wednesday, and Friday—for six solid months. We put her on prayer lists that literally circled the globe. People sent cards and notes, sometimes ten or more of them arriving in a single day's post. She bagged them all up and kept them in a closet, often pulling them out to read them when she was low, hurting, or discouraged.

And amazingly, God co-opted that enormously strong will that resided in Melissa, and He used it to help her battle her way through cancer with Scriptures on her mirror and praises in her heart. Through hair loss and physical weakness—daggers to a young woman who all her life had needed others' acceptance as well as a big time on Saturday night—she simply got tough and trusted God. By the time she'd completed her chemo program, she would say with a certain spunk in her voice: "He has taught me so much over the past year, and I really don't think I'd change a thing. I know He has allowed this cancer in my life for a reason, and if the only reason was to bring me closer to Him, then that's a good enough reason."

I'll be honest. That did not sound like my Melissa.

But it sure sounded good.

She had come through two of the most severe crisis situations a young woman can face in such a relatively short span of life. By thirty years of age, she had survived both an unmarried pregnancy and an unpredictable, deadly disease. And now more than ever, she was ready to keep fighting.

What we didn't know at the time was that other complications had already begun conspiring to take her down. And in less than three years, she just wouldn't have any fight left to give.

Overall Misconceptions

I don't know what others think when they hear that we've lost a grown daughter to suicide. I don't know what they think when they hear it about you and yours. Depending on how well they know either of us, of course, or how well they knew the person we loved, their opinions could range anywhere from detached and stereotypical to caring and curious. But no matter how closely they were acquainted to us or to them, they cannot possibly know the whole story and character of this person the way we do.

In some way, a little or a lot, they would be speaking from a misconception.

People hear suicide; they fill in the blanks. They build out ideas from their own experiences and knowledge. They think of others they know who went through a similar thing. They imagine how they would feel if it had happened to them. But what they don't do—what none of us ever do when we choose to construct quick judgments of others—is to capture the whole picture that helps interpret any isolated event or scenario. They fail to take into account the color and detail, the impressions and nuance, all the things that work together in any life to give that person, or that decision, or that outcome a context for understanding.

In order to find clues to Melissa's suicide, for example, one would need to be aware of these two other key experiences in her life: one that she brought on herself and one that just fell in her lap without any direct causation whatsoever. This doesn't mean her decision to kill herself was the appropriate response to the consequences and hardships she faced. But these major ordeals were obviously contributing factors, among many others, to the trajectory that led her toward desperation.

All I'm saying is that our deceased sons and daughters, wives and husbands, mothers and fathers, dear friends and relatives—they are more than that one tragic event. They are a composite of influences and situations and encounters and responses that all came together to form a life much larger than any carbon copies on a police report.

You and I know that.

But what happens sometimes in reacting to their death is that we, too—while never willing to shrink them down to where suicide is all we can see of them—can still fall victim to smudging our memories of them with misconceptions that fail to take their full lives into account, with misconceptions that stem from faulty religious belief, with misconceptions that keep us from healing the way God would desire for us.

I'm writing the rest of this chapter to help us all steer clear of that.

Does Suicide Condemn a Person to Hell?

The most notorious misconception about suicide is that anyone who takes his or her own life is destined for hell, that it automatically cuts them off from the grace of God, that they have committed the "unpardonable sin."

Yes, the Bible does speak of a sin (and it's not suicide, by the way) that is unforgivable: "blasphemy against the Spirit" (Matt. 12:31). Yet even this sin, when seen in context and alongside the whole counsel of Scripture, cannot refer to any one-time oath of doubt or defiance against the deity of God but to a complete, lifelong rejection of Him. "For God did not send His Son into the world that He might condemn the world, but that the world might be saved through Him" (John 3:17).

Many people, however, either believe or suspect that this misconception is true—that suicide does indeed seal the fate of the person who commits it. If you've been taught this, or if you've worried about it enough to convince yourself of its validity, then you need to search the Scriptures to find any evidence to support this claim. *I assure you, it is not there.* God never singles out the act of suicide as a "mortal sin," the way some faith traditions categorize it. If He did, then even the passing thought or attempt at killing oneself would qualify, for just as Jesus said the seeds of murder exist within every flash of anger (Matt. 5:21–22), so must the seeds of suicide live within every desire to carry it out.

I see in this misconception a perhaps unknowing effort to diminish God's nature and character—His power, wisdom, and love—viewing Him as narrow and legalistic, as though His own redemptive purposes could be taken out of His hands by the single act of an individual. It amounts to seeing God as small—small enough for us to figure Him out, to peg Him to the wall on a procedural point of order, forcing Him to dismiss any other reasoning in His sovereign plans that would otherwise have extended mercy toward this person.

Throughout history human pride has felt the need to sand down the undefined edges of God's activity. People feel more in control of things if they've properly codified His movements and know exactly where to walk so they can skirt safely around them. It's simply easier for mankind to place a hard equal sign between *suicide* and *eternal damnation* than to actually get to know God through His Word, through His Spirit, and through daily, surrendered relationship with Him.

So, there you go. Suicide sends people to hell.

Takes care of that problem.

But it also takes a lot of clear evidence out of the picture.

I ask you again: Why do you believe suicide is unforgivable? Who told you so? On what authority are you basing that view? Have you ever read it in the Bible?

No, here's what you'll find in the Bible: "Who can separate us from the love of Christ? Can affliction or anguish or persecution or famine or nakedness or sword? . . . For I am persuaded that not even death or life, angels or rulers, things present or things to come, hostile powers, height or depth, or any other created thing will have the power to separate us from the love of God that is in Christ Jesus our Lord!" (Rom. 8:35, 38–39).

Is suicide a sin? Yes, of course it is. The totality of Scripture leaves us no room to doubt that. It is a violation of the Sixth Commandment. It is not to be condoned and is worthy of punishment, as are all rebellious acts against God's law. In fact, we ourselves as surviving friends and family members can bear personal witness to what the consequences of this sin feel like, merely by standing within close range of those who took their own lives.

But if your loved one believed in Jesus and received the atonement of His blood for their sins, how could the results of one tragic moment condemn them to hell when God had already flung their sins—every last one of them—"as far as the east is from the west, so far has He removed our transgressions from us" (Ps. 103:12). "God proves His own love for us in that *while we were still sinners,* Christ died for us!" (Rom. 5:8, emphasis added).

God alone knows what occurred in our dear ones' hearts, all the way leading up to their death and all the way through it. And so we can pray what Abraham the patriarch prayed as he pled with God for the life of his nephew Lot, awash in the sin-infested city of Sodom: "Won't the Judge of all the earth do what is just?" (Gen. 18:25).

Yes, He will.

I feel sure you'll agree with me that if your son or daughter (or whatever relation applies in your case) were thinking clearly at the moment they carried out their final act, they would not have gone through with it. At some point a switch flipped in their minds, whether through the gradual wearing down of depression or despair, through the irrational logic of advanced anxiety, certainly through the chiding and goading of our great spiritual enemy. But they just finally lost touch with reality. They weren't thinking straight anymore.

And are we really to believe that our loving God, who had applied His Son's sacrifice to their sins, would angrily snatch back His promise at a time when this precious life had lost all rational bearings?

"Not even death" has the power "to separate us from the love of God."

Then why should this particular death do it?

Am I Wrong to Be Angry with God?

Another misconception about suicide and the extreme emotions involved in trying to heal from its aftermath touches on God's role in standing by and allowing this tragedy to happen. The heat of trauma and unexplainable loss can sometimes tempt you to lash out at Him in ways you might once have considered borderline blasphemy.

But search the Scriptures—particularly the psalms—and you will find many occasions when the people of God cried out to Him in angry, accusing tones: "How long will You forget me? Forever? How long will You hide Your face from me? How long will I store up anxious concerns within me, agony in my mind every day?" (Ps. 13:1–2). "Lord, how long will You look on?" (35:17). "God, how long will the enemy mock?" (74:10). "LORD—how long? Turn and have compassion on Your servants" (90:13).

The fact that such statements are printed in your Bible does not necessarily validate these outbursts as appropriate. But the fact that God in His wisdom preserved them in His holy Word indicates He does understand them and is not unnerved by them. He is not unaware why we might react this way.

And frankly, if there were ever a reason to incite desperate outrage in a person, it would be at the senseless loss of suicide, or the weariness of dealing with its endless threats, or amid the ongoing battles that simply will not end between you and a recalcitrant child or family member.

Most of us, especially those of us who are Christian, are basically hardwired to keep to ourselves any anger we feel toward God if we sense it rising up within us. And I'll admit, based on my own nature and my theological reasoning, I choose as a matter of conscience not to rail in anger against God when I'm upset about something. But if you were to ask me if I thought you would rile His temper by venting your anguish and frustrations in His direction, I would tell you to feel permission to go ahead. You would not be the first; you will not be the last. As I said even recently to someone who asked me a similar question, "Our God is a big God. He can take it."

As a parent, imperfect as I am, I've experienced what it's like for one of my children to be angry with me. Did it make me hate them? Did I deny them the right to speak with me? Of course not. When our girls were small and would have a tantrum about something, I usually knew what the underlying issues were. I understood what had led up to their frustration, what had caused their stack to blow. And I was generally aware of why I was on the receiving end of their displeasure. But did I consider their angry words to be grounds for disowning them? Would I not be there that night to tuck them into bed and pray with them, to check on them again before I'd settled down to sleep? I knew these weren't the last words I'd hear from them. I knew the day would come—probably very soon, perhaps as early as the next morning—when they'd see things a little differently and we could talk a bit more quietly.

That's because they're my kids. Just as we are God's

children. And soon they'd come back around and let me love on them. That's what families do.

And that's how we should view our life with God—bearing in mind, of course, the significant distinction that He is the rightful, all-powerful Ruler of the universe who has earned (unlike any earthly father) our complete fear, worship, and honor. Still, He has presented Himself to us as our heavenly Father and has chosen for us to relate to Him as His children. So this trauma we're working through in relation with Him is at its heart a family matter. And any father—of whom He is supreme—knows that his children will sometimes express anger and confusion and weariness and doubt. That's why a father often picks up his child, puts her in his lap, and says, "Honey, I know it hurts. I understand why this is breaking your heart. I agree with you that it's not fair. But I am here for you and will walk through this with you because I love you."

Healing comes within the circle of family love. And God is able to handle anything that happens within that relationship.

The fact is, taking your honest self to God, even with all its raw emotion and blinding grief, is exactly the place you need to take it. If the alternative is to dump your anger on others, especially in the form of indirect criticism and personal attack, you'll find much less to clean up later if you just pour it out in prayer to the One who can actually do something with it. If the alternative is to stow it all away in a hidden tank deep within your heart, afraid of offending God by speaking it aloud, then you're better off releasing the valve in frank communication with your heavenly Father than cramming all that pain and suffering into tight living quarters that will never be able to hold it.

God, mysterious as He is to our finite minds, is both transcendent and imminent. He is far above us and yet close at hand to us—no, *ever present* with us. As such, He knows the thoughts of our heart before we can even translate them into speech or action. So don't feel the need to run and hide from Him. Revere Him, yes. Praise Him, yes. Lay yourself prone before His awesome glory, yes, yes, yes.

But never think He is beyond involving Himself in the messy, moaning, misshapen realities that affect our every movement.

He can handle it.

No Easy Answers

I don't know everything. I don't know why Melissa would get involved with a man she hardly knew, putting herself in such a compromised situation as a nineteen-year-old girl. I don't know why the Lord allowed cancer to invade her little body or why I'll never enjoy the privilege of introducing her personally to my staff here in Nashville. They would have loved her; she would have loved them. I don't know why *you* are now required to soldier on through life, one person too light and yet with a heart that's twice as heavy.

I don't understand that.

I just know it's what's happened.

But we must not complicate our walk any further by loading it down with half-truths and unwarranted guilt. We can trust that God has not misplaced our children or disqualified them on a technicality. We can realize that for every emotional dead end we come to, every time our words play out and our hearts can't bear the silence, God is still there amid our hurts and fears. He is willing just to sit with us in our grief and not judge us for being so lost about what to do.

I have counseled many people through the crucible of suicide in my decades of pastoring, and I have never known anyone who simply woke up one morning and decided this was the last day they wanted to live. You and I understand better than anyone that the final act of suicide is but a weary end to months and years of agonizing struggle. The decisions and events that set the stage for this tragic conclusion could not be unraveled or understood if that's all we ever did for the rest of our lives. The nature of suicide is characterized by complexity.

So I warn you to be careful around people who, even in meaning well, can make such trite, unthinking statements about you, your loved one, and your family. Simplistic reasoning and solutions will never suffice to give us comfort. More likely, they will only confuse or frustrate us. Our safest place to stand is within the Word of God, being nurtured by the gentle Spirit of God, receiving daily assurance that the only One who can sift through the intricate details of our situation and infuse them with meaning and purpose is the One we're already trusting for everything else. In Him, the Bible says, is life's "fountain" of truth and wisdom. "In Your light we will see light" (Ps. 36:9).

Truly in Him, there is no misconception.

We will no longer be little children, tossed by the waves and blown around by every wind of teaching, by human cunning with cleverness in the techniques of deceit. But speaking the truth in love, let us grow in every way into Him who is the head—Christ.
EPHESIANS 4:14–15

A Letter to You

if you're contemplating suicide

I imagine a lot of people have given you a lot of advice over the years. Some in anger, some in superiority, some in exasperation, some without knowing at all what they're even talking about. They are usually only trying to help, and you'd probably admit that you'd have been smart to follow some of what they said. But at the same time, a good bit of people's opinions can be simplistic and overgeneralized. That's true.

One thing I've heard, for example (and, honestly, have thought sometimes), is that "suicide is the most selfish of all actions." Here you think you're doing what you need to do to cope with your own problems and get out of everyone's way, but suicide ultimately leaves all the burden on others—to deal with their mental images, to upset their lives and schedules, to invite unwanted attention to their family problems, to impact their work, to haunt their dreams. You, on the other hand—you're out. You're free. It's not your problem anymore.

Let's be honest, there's some truth to that accusation. And I feel sure there's a time and place when this kind of straight talk is exactly what's needed. But right now, right here, I'm agreeing with you that this "selfish" angle is in many ways a misconception. I believe my Melissa, though she was certainly trying to escape her consequences, knew she had caused her husband and family a lot of trouble. I don't think she found it hard to convince herself that it was best for everybody, all the way around, if she was just gone.

I've known others who had committed such grievous acts—habits, passions, and weaknesses that had cost them so much loss of trust by their families—they just couldn't bear to see the ones they loved suffering any longer as a result of this. They looked into the mirror and saw a monster, a person they could hardly recognize, a person who had stupidly lost sight of what really mattered in life. And they just didn't want anyone else having to put up with that face, with that memory of rejection or disloyalty, not for one more day.

What I'm saying is, I don't think you interpret your suicidal thoughts as being selfish. It's never quite as simple as that. But I do think you're trying to solve with death what can best be solved—even if quite painfully so—with your life.

Each of us, if we're wise, will finally arrive at the place where we see that all the energy we invest into impressing others, or in trying to be perfect, or in getting people to notice us and like us is really a waste of time—a misplaced concern—because others will eventually see our flaws. I mean, even if we're doing everything *right*, some people will choose to be disapproving of us. But when we fail to live up to expectations—when we realize we're not the people we intended to be, that this is not the life we foresaw for ourselves—then we'll be at a crossroads of decision. Do we despair of our failure and bail out on life? Do we rev up the approval machine and try showing everybody we're better than they know? Or do we let these failings and blemishes and broken promises become a backdrop to fulfill our actual purpose in life—to show forth the greatness of our God and His love?

The Lord said through the prophet Jeremiah, "The wise man must not boast in his wisdom; the strong man must not boast in his strength; the wealthy man must not boast in his wealth. But the one who boasts should boast in this, that he understands and knows Me" (Jer. 9:23–24). "The one who boasts," Paul said, "must boast in the Lord" (1 Cor. 1:31).

Like most of us, you may have always wanted to impress others with your winning personality, your physical strength, your technical skill, your strong character. But maybe when that didn't work, what you failed to realize is that God is "not impressed by the strength of a horse; He does not value the power of a man. The LORD values those who fear Him, those who put their hope in His faithful love" (Ps. 147:10–11). His "power is perfected in weakness" (2 Cor. 12:9). He can do more with your broken life than you would ever have let Him do with your intact one.

And when you boil it all down, that's what ultimately makes the most important impression on everybody.

What if the best thing you could do for your family, instead of quitting on them to avoid further embarrassment, was to say: "I will not be afraid to admit what I've done. It was wrong. I know it. I am truly sorry. And I promise you, whatever it takes, I will not keep living this way. But because I know—and *you* know—that I am incapable of correcting these problems and issues by myself, then when you see lasting changes in me, there will be only one explanation. You will know who is behind it.

It will be Christ's power in me. And I don't want you to miss seeing that. I don't want you to miss seeing what He can do."

Think about that.

Prove to your family that you're not a selfish person. Prove to yourself that you're more valuable alive. And God will prove that you have a generation-changing purpose in being here: to watch Him do His restorative work through you.

> *Therefore, I will most gladly boast all the more about my weaknesses, so that Christ's power may reside in me. So I take pleasure in weaknesses, insults, catastrophes, persecutions, and in pressures, because of Christ. For when I am weak, then I am strong.*
> 2 Corinthians 12:9–10

CHAPTER 5

Drugs and Depression

*T*hings we don't completely understand:

Suicide. Every inclination in the human mind is to preserve one's own life. You graze against a hot bulb while you're cleaning the light fixtures in your bathroom, and you yank your hand away. Pure reflex. You stumble walking down a flight of stairs, and you grab the handrail, you attempt to correct, anything to keep from completely losing your balance and risking six weeks in a boot cast.

The only variation to this rule is the mother-bear mentality that kicks in when someone's child is in danger, or the soldier's battle instinct that thrusts him forward in defense of his unit. When a firefighter or police officer places himself in life-threatening peril, or when an average citizen rushes a gun-wielding attacker in public, we recognize the nobility and bravery in that.

They push past the self-preservation urge in order to attempt a greater rescue.

But suicide? It makes no sense to the thinking mind. It goes against nature and impulse. Only in one's utter desperation is this anomaly able somehow to contort itself into a shape that fits on the same grid with normal life processes. Otherwise, it's something we would always run away from, never toward. Suicide is hard to understand. So is . . .

Medicine. You may feel a headache coming on mid-morning, and as a precaution against feeling it worsen through the day, you might take an aspirin to knock down the pain. But unless you're a trained nurse, doctor, or pharmacist, you probably have no idea how that little tablet or capsule interacts with blood vessels and body chemistry to alleviate your symptoms. All you know is that you take one, and you look up an hour later and realize your headache is gone. You don't have to understand why.

Depression. Perhaps you battle it within yourself: the low moods, the troubled sleeping patterns, the loss of energy, the diminished ability to concentrate, or any combination of related impediments. Perhaps it's your child or spouse who tends to gravitate toward it, or who is absolutely consumed by it, and you're the one who tries to navigate and talk them through, the one who tries to figure out the right balance of patience, prodding, and quiet that helps them cope, without allowing the necessary demands of everyday life to go consistently unmet. Yet even if you're quite familiar with the feelings and indicators of depression, it is probably still a great mystery in your life—how

it happens, what causes it, how to counteract it. Most of us fail
to understand.

But one thing we do understand. These three—suicide,
drugs, and depression—often travel in a pack. And if we intend
to prevent them from leading to deadly conclusions in the lives
of those we love, as well as in our own, we need to understand
them better.

I'll dare say that if you've lost a child, mate, parent, or friend
to suicide, a mixture of drugs and depression was involved in
it. And even as you try to rebuild from the grief and loneliness,
you may begin to see these same ingredients lining up in your
own life, luring you away unwittingly from the most complete
experience of healing possible.

So this chapter is a warning. A reminder. A primer of lessons
we can learn.

It's an attempt to understand.

The Drug Question

I need to say right up front, before discussing my views
on prescription drugs, that I am not a physician. So any medical opinions of mine should be weighed alongside those who
possess competencies in their particular fields. I have come to
my conclusions based on much personal experience and observation, and I do feel strongly about these matters. But before
heeding my advice—especially since I cannot be specifically
aware of your situation—you should fold it in with other counsel you have received from those who know you best.

One of the most common questions I'm asked, whenever the
issue of antidepressants and antianxiety medication is brought

up, is whether I'm opposed to their use, if I feel as though a person is *wrong* to take them. My answer is a definite no.

As prescribed.

As needed.

But what so often happens in a rampant drug culture like ours is that the ready availability of these drugs, the ease with which doctors prescribe them, and the tendency of individuals to become dependent on them lead to long-term, largely unsupervised self-treatment of depressive symptoms that is usually (in my opinion) too extreme in relation to the actual target problem.

These are powerful medications we're talking about. And most people receive them from their family doctor, who may or may not be as studied on their effects and proper usages as someone in the psychiatric field would tend to be. Furthermore, these general practitioners and internists may be simply responding to a spoken request from their patients, made in a few minutes of checkup conversation in the examination room, not after the kind of careful thinking and questioning that should logically precede such an adjustment to a person's overall medical program.

These doctors won't say it for the record, but I've asked them—quite a few of them—and they've nearly all admitted to me: they overprescribe these drugs. It's a way of getting people out the door with a "happy pill" that (as long as one's head is planted firmly in the sand) is considered to be a fairly harmless, inconsequential risk to their mental or physical health. *What's the big deal? We'll watch it.*

But they don't in many cases. They don't really know these people. They don't really know what's going on in their lives.

They don't have time, or frankly the jurisdiction and responsibility, to analyze properly a patient's overall mental state. But by pulling out their prescription pad and introducing into a person's system a new medication that likely has little or nothing to do with one's observable physical condition, these doctors *assume* responsibility for the outcome. And when these medicines are allowed to be refilled again and again, or adjusted to another version of drug when the first one doesn't satisfy the patient's needs, these doctors help create a runaway situation that just invites unintended consequences.

OB-GYNs, too, frequently prescribe these types of drugs, not just for postpartum issues but for women at any stage of life who are struggling and stressed. They say they feel run down, they feel listless, they feel agitated, they feel nervous, and so the doctor responds, "Let me give you something that can help." It's often the first step to needing more and more drug usage in order to function.

Let me go back, though, to my original statement: No, I don't think it's wrong to use these drugs at certain times for temporary relief. Many people who have come to me in search of pastoral counseling over the years say, "I just feel like I need something to get me over the hump, to help me get through this crisis, to take the edge off until I can get back to normal." And I understand that. In my view the well-controlled application of an inhibitor of some sort in that situation can often steady a person long enough until other, more natural sources of help can begin to take over.

But again, my experience tells me that this "magic" method of healing is overadvertised and overused. I honestly don't think I would be exaggerating—not by much anyway—to say that more than half of my church, when I was pastor, was on some form of antidepressant or antianxiety drug. And I'm sure this same metric goes for churches and neighborhoods and workplaces all around the country. By any definition it is out of control. This many people—even with as many problems as we face today—simply cannot require, indisputably, this high level of medicinal intervention. Just can't.

Melissa was one who cycled in and out of doctor's offices and mental health clinics throughout much of her adult life. Doctor shopping, they call it. And though I understand efforts are being made in the medical community to help them be able to see everything a patient is being treated for, even by other physicians, Melissa made the rounds to acquire multiple, conflicting prescriptions for her various ailments, both physical and emotional. I'm sure it's still done by many, even with these precautions in place.

Which introduces a related topic: *prescription pain medication.*

When I mentioned in the previous chapter that Melissa, having successfully defeated cancer, was struggling with another debilitating hazard, I was referring to this potent combination of antidepressants, antianxiety meds, and prescription pain pills that was encouraged during her chemo treatments. It had a profound reaction with the addictive side of her personality. Issues that had significantly subsided in her life through her mid- to later twenties suddenly came roaring back, even after her lymphoma had been summarily defeated. We could see the signs. Her husband could certainly see them. They were hard to miss.

Melissa reached the point where she was actually buying prescription pills off the street. I know it sounds like the stuff of urban movie backdrops, but trust me, you can find certain areas in just about any town, where if you drive through late at night, making the right kind of muted signals, a dealer will appear at your window with assortments of whatever you want. Melissa did that.

And while I wasn't as keenly aware of her drug use myself, not living with her every day, I certainly had no trouble recognizing that her behavior was becoming more and more bizarre and affected. As it turned out, her mental health professional had recently adjusted some of her medications, which had resulted in this drastic, noticeable change of mood and conduct. I finally went to her—this was no more than three weeks before her death—and said, "Melissa, honey, something is bad wrong. You need to be in the hospital. Whatever you're on, whatever's going on . . ."

"I'm *FINE!*" she shot back.

"Melissa," I said, "your daddy loves you better than anybody in the world, and your daddy *knows* you better than anybody in the world. I know when things are not right, and I'm telling you, honey, something is not right."

"I'm *FINE!*" she repeated. "My *doctor* says I'm fine."

"Well, will you tell your doctor that your *father* said you need help, that you need to be admitted to the hospital?"

She didn't tell him anything. What she did was to come back to me with a note, purportedly from her doctor, that said she did *not* require hospitalization. "See?" But looking at it more carefully later, I could tell the piece of paper she'd given me was inscribed in her own handwriting. She had forged it.

The drugs changed her.

I don't mind telling you that after her death I secured a lawyer to look into whether or not Melissa's psychiatrist had overmedicated her or had acted improperly in his recommendations for her care without appropriate counsel from others. I had an investigator go through his records, just to see. I'm not a lawsuit kind of person—I'd never sued anybody in my life—and I didn't end up suing him either because nothing really turned up. But no one will ever be able to convince me that the interaction of these medications on Melissa's mental faculties did not contribute to her inexplicable behavior and her eventual suicide.

They are connected—drugs, depression, and suicide. Not that they're *always* connected. But they are connected enough that we need to be very careful how we manage our medical life as well as those under our watch who take medicines for their mental or physical needs, even when the doctor instructs it.

Toward Total Health and Healing

I realize, depending on your situation, depending at what point you find yourself as you're reading this, that the observations I've just made could strike you as harsh and unsympathetic. I hope not. Obviously, if you've endured the suicide of one of your close family members, I can relate to much of what you feel. Even though I'm a religious leader by day and night, a man of deep faith, someone who's often been counted on to be strong and decisive in times of heated crisis, I am no superman. Melissa's death, now several years' distant at this writing, still grips me at times with heavy hands. It is not a stretch for me to see how anyone who experiences the throes of grief that you and I share could need medicinal assistance to tide them over. This is extreme suffering of a unique order, and it calls for maximum-strength endurance to walk it through.

I do understand. Surely you believe me.

And as I hopefully stated clearly enough, I am not a voice that speaks out against drug usage of every kind. If you hear someone endorsing that approach, someone who's so exclusive in their thinking that they overlook the very personal, case-by-case dynamics that factor into an individual's medical decisions, you should not receive their condemnation as a guilt inducer. There is room for open discussion and dialogue on this subject and a relatively wide berth for specific, healthy opinions and applications.

But as you pilot yourself through this delicate maze of emotions, I would simply counsel you to consider one bit of caution, a wide-angle perspective that I believe helps us keep our larger goals in view while we manage the day-to-day challenges that sometimes are all we can see.

It's this: I fear that an *overuse* of psychotropic drugs typically produces a short-circuiting of the emotional and mental growth that is capable of occurring without them.

Want to read that again?

Let me say it another way: the qualities that exist within antidepressants and antianxiety drugs to help us cope with emotional distress can also, over time, disorient our senses so that we do not deal properly and completely with the issues that are before us.

It can slow down our healing process.

You know, for example, if you read the fine print carefully enough or listen to the fast-talking announcer on the radio and television commercials, that some of the admitted side effects of these anxiety medications are suicidal thoughts and tendencies. The drugs you take (the drugs your children are perhaps taking) to help fend off depression and nerves can often exacerbate the moods and apprehensions you're trying to neutralize.

What's more, as I've already alluded to, many of the physicians who prescribe these medicines for patients like us are motivated, if not by a strain of activism, at least by a heart of compassion. They see us hurting so badly, trying to hold ourselves together, and they feel sorry for us, which can encourage them to overcompensate in order to help us. But again, they may do so without fully grasping all the issues involved—emotionally, relationally, mentally, spiritually. If you start ingesting medicines long-term that your body has never had a history of responding to, especially amid the intensity of deep anguish and stress, then you don't know what kind of personality changes it could invoke. Attach them to a temperament like our Melissa's, and they're like a loaded gun in your hand.

Each of us is familiar with real-life scenarios and sermon illustrations that show how our well-meaning attempts at comforting and consoling people can sometimes in the end do them more harm than good. Often by bravely working through our difficulties, facing them head-on, and receiving the active ministry of God's care and comfort (and the ministry of His people), we grow the muscles we need for surviving our suffering and becoming useful in serving others who are equally in need.

Can prescription medicines participate effectively in this course of healing? Absolutely yes. But—here's what I truly think—overusing them, using them too long, and using them as a *replacement* rather than a *partner* in the coping experience creates an artificial healing that is less likely to respond well to upcoming points of crisis when they arise (which they will).

I want to see you heal well from this violent wound to your heart.

I want to see your children and loved ones grow strong, not dependent.

I want to see both of us coming through this, not merely skirting around it. But doing that will require some sound wisdom, some forced effort, some strong new habits.

And new understanding.

Depression and Mental Illness

Preventing suicide almost always involves closing the loop on depression. This is the one consistent link that is nearly synonymous with suicidal intentions. So whether we're talking about a person in our life who is showing all the signs of withdrawing from human interaction or whether we're talking about a condition that is personally pulling us under as we attempt to rise above this tragedy, the task of understanding what depression is (and what it is not) is an important field of study for us. We need to be able to frame up our lives in such a way that we can respond with strength to what depression seeks to impose on us and our loved ones.

With a college degree in psychology and a PhD in ethics, I've spent a great deal of time studying various moral and psychological issues, including the nature of mental illness. Not all depression, of course, can be classified in this way; some of it is more cyclical or directly tied to particular events or episodes. But I believe by considering the following observations on mental disorders, we can avoid certain misunderstandings about depression and learn how to live in freedom and victory over it.

1. Most mental illness has nothing to do with poor character or upbringing. While personal flaws and serious parenting mistakes can cause a wide number of difficulties for anyone, mental problems can also hound those who have tremendous integrity and back stories, people who were reared in fine homes where the parents were extremely devoted, loving, and caring. You simply cannot typecast a depressed individual as a person of bad, lazy character. And you as a parent, if your child struggles with depression, should not beat yourself to death as the *de facto* source behind their problems. You're not claiming perfection, but neither should you feel cloaked in unwarranted blame. You are here to help this person and to help yourself, not to be distracted by others' judgments.

2. Those with mental illness can be misunderstood even by churches, Christian friends, and family. I wish this were not true. It shouldn't be true. But plenty of personal experience exists to suggest that the Christian community can often fail to understand the intricacies of emotional problems or be patient with those who struggle with them. Some people are too quickly critical, overly simplistic, attempting to characterize depression as purely a spiritual issue. Does depression contain spiritual elements? Of course. Everything does. Can it be aggravated by spiritual doubts or by resisting relationship with God?

Of course. Everything can. But we as Christians need to realize that those who battle depression do so for a variety of reasons, many of which they cannot just "snap out of." I don't say this as a slam against the church; I say it as a challenge for us to be more understanding and patient with those who wrestle against difficult mental issues and to challenge those who know depression firsthand to share with others from their experience so the church can become a more trusted, effective, and safe haven for the emotionally impaired.

3. Mental illness can be affected by demonic activity. Based on my experience—what I've witnessed—I believe demonic *possession* is a rare occurrence, even though the casting out of demons was a fairly frequent emphasis of Jesus' ministry and mission. Yet it is not unheard of, even in our day, odd as its manifestations may seem. Much more common, however, is the experience of demonic *subjection* (to borrow a term from the late theologian John Newport), not only in mental illness but in all kinds of personal struggles. By this I mean we are able to subject certain areas of our lives to Satan's control, thereby providing him free rein through our poor choices to build up pockets of resistance and confusion in our hearts and minds. We looked at this theme in the chapter on spiritual warfare in terms of "strongholds." That's how the Bible describes those places where we allow the enemy to wall off our beliefs and behaviors from allegiance to God. If we insist on being bitter, for example, or believing unbiblical lies about God and ourselves, or participating in sexual impurity and other activities that coarsen the conscience—to name only a few—we leave ourselves particularly exposed to certain temptations and distorted ways of thinking. Our failure to let Christ rule in any of these areas can open us up to being hardened and muddled in mind, subject to guilt, discouragement, hopelessness . . . depression.

4. *Mental illness can cause breaks with reality that absolve such individuals from full responsibility for their actions.* The Bible endorses an ethic of personal responsibility that calls all people to accountability for their actions. We consider this stance to be integral to the strength of our society, the health of our families, and the proper governance of our individual lives. However, Scripture also contains multiple examples that describe how the presence of extenuating circumstances, lack of knowledge, or unavoidable negligence can either reduce or eliminate a person's responsibility for what they did. Leviticus 4:22–26, for example, prescribes a sacrificial alternative for a person who "unintentionally violates" any of the commands of God. Carrying this principle forward, I believe one's mental health can deteriorate to such an advanced state that the affected person is no longer fully in charge of their decision-making faculties. Only the Lord knows, of course, when that line is crossed. But we can be nearly 100 percent assured that the one we loved who took his or her own life was on the other side of that threshold. Depression has the power to take us to places we never imagined we'd go.

I could keep on, but I don't intend to make this a dissertation on the subject. I mainly want to comfort you with the fact that if depression is a major element in your life or family—if it's what you're currently forced to consider as a "normal" part of your everyday living—you should not be made to feel that overcoming it or helping another person through it is as simple as making Dr. Phil adjustments. Depression is truly complex, not just in your mind but in reality. It is not automatically indicative of personal weakness; in truth, it may not signify a specific weakness of yours at all. The fact that you're battling so hard against it could just as reasonably confirm the toughness of your inner strength.

So fight it, yes, with prayer, with trusted friends and counsel, with healthy accountability, with careful habits, with controlled disciplines, with physical fitness, with sound medical advice—with everything you've got—with even *more* than you've got because God is fighting for you. But do not add to its already existing pressure by convincing yourself that you're a failure and a lost cause. This is no piece of cake. You've been through enough hardship and loss to splay anyone's nerves and gumption. Get up in the morning knowing "His mercies . . . are new" (Lam. 3:22–23) and that you are not alone.

A whole lot of us understand.

Recovering at the Speed of Sound Advice

If I could leave you with one message in regard to the prescription drug issue: *be slow*. Particularly in regard to your children and teenagers—even young adult children who look to you for counsel and advice—gather a full range of opinions before deciding that medicinal treatments are your best way of dealing with depression and emotional disturbances.

I realize that certain mental illnesses can reach a depth that requires ongoing medical therapy. Some situations have devolved to the level of psychosis and are too serious to manage any other way. But the vast majority of depressive issues—what could more accurately be categorized as *neuroses*—can likely be managed better with only light touches (if any) from inhibitor drugs.

For one thing, many of these medications are difficult to quit. You don't just decide, "Hey, I think I've had enough now," and then put them away. The protocol for coming down from these prescription drug regimens involves a weaning process. It's complicated. It's serious. It's anything but easy in many cases. And even though a wide number of physicians tout these medicines as almost magic bullets to make the bad moods disappear, these drugs can frequently cause new problems while trying to solve another. Like I said, Melissa popped them like candy, with most of them being pushed at her by the doctors and psychiatrists she saw. But her innate personality type, like that of many others you see on television who have landed in rehab centers, proved a poisonous combination. In the end it proved deadly.

When it comes to making medical decisions involving emotional concerns, both for yourself and for others, take it slowly. Widen your sample size of available advisors. And be careful.

Seek to understand.

Finally, as far as depression itself goes, don't be ashamed to admit you're struggling. If some people don't understand—your parents perhaps, your siblings, certain friends and acquaintances—try not to let their dismissive or condescending attitudes drive you underground in guilt and despondency. Find help from those who will listen, who won't immediately judge, who are truly grounded in God's Word, and who have helped others like you long-term with proven results.

Let them grow your understanding.

Don't jump for quick fixes as a means of escape from your suffering or sadness, but rather allow God to build you back slowly and gradually, steadily and comprehensively. His healing methods often travel at a speed less brisk than we would like but not because He can't go any faster or doesn't care how long it takes for us to feel better again. He simply knows we heal best in strong, cumulative stages than in leaps and bounds that can leave too many foundational matters overlooked and untouched. Trust His heart and His timing. Believe who He says you are and what His Word promises to those who wait on Him. Others may be waiting impatiently on you to get better, but you will be your best for them in the long run if you heal in full proportions.

Understand that.

Drugs, depression, and suicide. Wherever they've come together to wound us, may God take them apart and put us back together as people who are more whole because we've been broken. Because we know what wholeness truly costs and means.

> *I lift my eyes toward the mountains.*
> *Where will my help come from?*
> *My help comes from the LORD,*
> *the Maker of heaven and earth.*
> PSALM 121:1–2

A Letter to You

if you're contemplating suicide

If I could guess how you might feel today—how *life* feels to you—the phrase *going downhill* comes to mind. The world seems to be falling out from under you. The road back up to happiness and confidence appears longer and more impossible than it did perhaps even a few days or months ago.

Does that come close to describing it?

And I'd be lying if I told you that by this time next week, you'd realistically be back up near the top where you want to be. You're probably correct in thinking there's a lot of ground to cover, even if your family and friends are supportive, even if nothing unforeseen happens that could take you down another peg. This will need to be a patient walk. I hope that's not discouraging to you.

But most real health and healing, as I just shared in this chapter, is usually accomplished in measured steps, the kind where you don't lunge haphazardly ahead and put yourself at risk of a steeper fall, but instead where you gather your full body weight firmly on each progressive rung so you can keep stepping up with increasing, proven confidence.

If you knew there was a way to climb out of this darkness and be more likely to stay at a consistently better place, wouldn't you be willing to go at a speed that held out the most promise of that?

I honestly believe you would.

If you knew there was another way besides suicide that

could leave you feeling in control and living with more hope, wouldn't you be willing to alter your way of thinking?

I believe you would.

I don't know if you're on medication right now to help you stay up on the higher elevations. The right form of medical help can often be a good way to scale some of the steepest ground. But maybe it's time to consider slowly releasing your dependence on that. Maybe as much as you count on that drug to keep you out of the depths, it's actually one of the reasons being "up" doesn't often feel very secure or doesn't stay that way for long.

As I said earlier in the chapter, any changes you choose to make to your medical program or prescription drug usage should be done with the counsel of people who understand you best and can speak most knowledgeably to your situation. I'm not suggesting *in any way* that you act on my advice out of context with other views, especially those who possess specific awareness of what's going on in your life. Please hear me on that.

All I know is that I can still hear my daughter saying, "I'm *FINE!*" that squeaky voice rising both in pitch and volume. I can hear it right now, even as I'm talking to you. It pierces through me. But she *wasn't* fine. Or anywhere close to fine. And while she obviously was overusing—abusing—I believe her story might have been different if she had allowed God and her friends and family to help bring her along slowly, more steadily, more healthily, building emotional strength day by day, step-by-step, until the ups and downs didn't feel so wild and unstable.

I'd imagine right now, too, depression is probably tugging down really hard on you. It can be so difficult to counteract its pull. Maybe on some days, maybe through a whole stretch of days, you make good progress against it. But then it shows up again with such a growl and fury and heavy undertow, it can take you down as low as ever.

Just because I'm a preacher, don't hear me saying that you're *bad* or *weak* for not being able to overcome its resistance every day. Depression is hard. Hard? No, *hard* doesn't really capture it. I don't know *any* word that can capture it. But I know from what I've walked through myself and what I've seen in others, there is a way up from downhill. And the higher you climb with the same people and tools that will still be with you at the top, the cleaner and stronger and more loved you will feel.

The theme of this chapter was "understanding"—trying to understand things that often make no sense, looking at hard problems in a different light, learning how growth and recovery happen when God is in the center of it. And while this doesn't mean there's only one specific way for your life to feel better than it does now, it does mean you have options you probably haven't considered. So please don't give up on something you haven't tried. Don't lose sight of yourself at a better place. Listen to the people who really love you, who really know you—especially the people who really know God. And ask them to help you start rebuilding—slowly, guardedly, carefully, patiently—until you're stronger than ever. Until you can even help other people who've lost their way.

I will say to God, my rock, "Why have You forgotten me? Why must I go about in sorrow because of the enemy's oppression?" My adversaries taunt me, as if crushing my bones, while all day long they say to me, "Where is your God?" Why am I so depressed? Why this turmoil within me? Put your hope in God, for I will still praise Him, my Savior and my God.

PSALM 42:9–11

CHAPTER 6

The Primal Cry

*A*s far as I know, I was the last person Melissa ever spoke to. Not long before I received the phone call from her neighbor, reporting the sudden appearance of emergency vehicles at the house, Melissa had already called me that morning. Her voice was unlike her. Hard to describe. A bit deeper than usual. Cold, raspy, dispassionate, detached. Almost a monotone. Devoid of all light and feeling. Heavy. Gone.

"Daddy," she said, without any of the usual, opening pleasantries, "I just, uh . . . I just want to tell you I love you."

"Well . . . thank you, honey. I love you too."

A pause.

Did she want something?

"Tell Mom and the girls I love them."

Odd.

I almost said, "OK, sure," but then quickly thought better of it, landing on something else—anything to try drawing her out, to arouse a response, to jolt her out of her stupor: "No, honey," I said, "*you* tell them."

"Nooo," she replied, barely above a whisper. This was taking effort. To concentrate on the next thought, the next sentence, was seemingly herculean, beyond her strength.

Next came a deep, sad breath. "I can't, Daddy. Just tell them for me."

"*You* tell them, Melissa. Please, honey—"

"Daddy . . ."

How that word hung in the air, even after the phone had clicked and disconnected from the other end, humming for a short moment in mechanical silence, then returning to a steady dial tone.

"Daddy, I love you . . ."

That was it.

"Daddy, I love you . . ."

That was all.

The last words I'd ever hear from her.

——— ——— ———

She had said something similar to me a couple of months earlier, when I had informed her that her mother and I would be moving away soon, that I had taken a new position in Atlanta. The sadness had darkened instantly across her face, much more harshly than it should, or at least more than I expected. After all, we would only be two and a half hours away—not as though we'd be unable to come back and visit the girls and their families on a fairly frequent basis. Perhaps even more than they'd like us to! But for a reason I could not quite interpret fully at the time, the thought of our leaving dealt a sharp, sudden blow to her heart, upsetting her at a deep, tender place.

And just like on the morning of her death, her words—while kind and affirming in a strict, literal sense—left behind a haunting, disturbing air.

"You *can't* move away, Daddy," she said. "You're my *rock*."

"Melissa . . ."

"It's true," she kept on. "Allison and Laura, they have their husbands. They have what they need. But you—you're my rock."

"You have *Thomas*, honey," I corrected her. "You know how much he loves you."

"I know, Daddy, but . . . you just don't . . . it's just not the same. I *need* you here. You're my rock."

How ironic. This was the same young woman who as a girl, as a teenager, as a youthful adult, would get so angry with me—and would *stay* angry for days, for weeks at a time, boiling over at every attempt I made to help draw loving boundaries around her. I don't know how many times through the years I would've *craved* hearing her tell me how strongly she sensed my love for her, how safe I made her feel, how deeply she knew she could count on me. And yet hearing it on this day, in this frantic tone of voice, when she rightly should have been looking to her husband—and to her God—for that kind of support and anchoring, this statement of hers just throttled me with worry.

Besides, I had another reason—a secret reason—for being leery of it.

Even though Melissa had never threatened suicide, as far as I knew, and had certainly never *attempted* suicide beyond maybe what we all considered a few attention-getting gestures, the Lord (I now believe) had given me three distinct dreams over a relatively short period of time—dreams in which I had seen Melissa's little body lying dead in a casket. At each occurrence I would awaken startled—shaken, frightened. Yet I dared not tell anyone else. After all, it was just a dream. How far can you take that? Why worry my wife and others needlessly with something so amorphous? So I did my best to chalk it up to a father's latent fears, even though worrying and being nervous about Melissa was an emotion not unknown to me, having so often sat at home over the years, wondering where she was, fearing what would become of her.

Please, Lord, not this . . .

"Daddy, I love you."

"Daddy, you're my rock."

That's not what she had said to me on the weekend preceding her death, during perhaps the most bizarre episode Dayle and I had ever witnessed in relation to Melissa. She and her mother had spent what should have been a wonderful time enjoying a local theater production. But after returning to Melissa's house following the show, tensions had somehow escalated—over something—to the point that she actually held my wife hostage in her home. Only by coming to Dayle's aid and physically prying her loose from Melissa's clutches was I able to usher her safely away.

While my wife was not in danger, she was deeply concerned about Melissa's erratic behavior and the escalation of symptoms, which clearly revealed Melissa's change in emotional state. We didn't know exactly what this meant or from what depths of torment it had arisen, except that Melissa was obviously in desperate need of accelerated, immediate help. When the time became appropriate to speak of it again following this troubling event, I begged her to please consult her therapist about hospitalization.

But nothing was getting through. We seemed to be losing her again.

"Daddy, I love you."

"Daddy, you're my rock."

Oh, Melissa.

At some point in the ensuing week, she had told Renée, my former secretary, "I know what I did to my parents the other night was wrong, and I owe them both an apology. But I'm still not going over there for Thanksgiving."

"Melissa," Renée said, "what does your Daddy want more than anything in the world? He just wants his family there with him. He wants to have a happy day together with all of you."

"I know, I know," she sighed.

Renée waited to see what might hopefully follow.

"I'm probably going," Melissa finally said, yet was careful to add, "but I'm not going to tell them ahead of time that I'm coming. I'll just show up."

I am so, so glad she did.

——— ——— ———

When I realized Melissa had disengaged the phone, I immediately began calling her back. Again and again. No answer.

I started texting. That was actually her preferred form of remote communication.

Still, no response.

I tried calling Thomas, too, on *his* cell phone, knowing he was off work and accessible for the holiday weekend. But nothing came back. I couldn't get anybody.

Stopping, waiting, praying—checking the phone again—still waiting—convinced of her imminent danger, while at the same time trying to assure myself that I was probably overreacting.

"That's just Melissa." How many times over the years had I thought or said that? I hoped and prayed now that it was really true.

But what should I do? Should I do something?

Dayle was on the road. She had left early that morning, headed for Atlanta, having scheduled an appointment with a realtor who had selected a number of houses to show her, while I stayed back to work on the yard, the leaves, and the bushes—the curb appeal of the house in Greenville we needed to sell.

And I had just about succeeded at calming myself down when the other phone call arrived, the one from her neighbor. Yes, something had happened all right. Something was wrong. I tore off toward her house, but upon arriving was told by a waiting police officer that I should hurry to the hospital. They had taken Melissa there.

Identifying myself at the front desk, I was ushered to a private waiting room and told that someone would be down very soon to update me on her condition.

How many times had I been inside this very hospital as a pastor? How many times had I been the one doing the comforting? My mind would just not stop spinning. Frantic. How much longer until I knew something? Anything.

Pacing, praying, hoping. Shortly the door opened. A young female doctor entered.

And I could tell. Inside I already knew. Melissa was gone.

"Daddy, I love you."

Melissa, why? Why, Melissa?

"Daddy, you're my rock."

No, I'm not.

I never felt less strong and stable than I did at that moment, in that little room, sitting there in the quiet with my grief, all by myself. *What am I going to tell Dayle? How in the world am I going to tell my girls?*

But I can tell you this: *my* Rock was there in that little room. As surely as the dense haze of grief began to envelop me, rapidly, so did the ready memory of God's Word and the faithful cloud of His presence. I was hurting so badly—*so* badly—but I could feel Him so close.

I sank hard to one knee, then to the other . . . and the Scriptures just came. Not from me but from Him. Floating in on the mists of trusted memory.

"The LORD gave, and the LORD hath taken away . . ." the words of Job (1:21 KJV) descended around my shoulders with such heavy, awful truth. And yet it was still truth. It was truth just the same—truth that remains strong even when life is so terribly bad.

"The LORD gave, and the LORD hath taken away; blessed be the name of the LORD."

The Many Moods of Grief

Grief.

It is primal.

The primal cry.

Of all the dissimilarities in our personal stories of tragedy, this one element is surely the most universal: the deep, guttural pain of immediate loss. For me it felt like going numb—just a shrouding thickness in the air, making it hard to feel or breathe or focus. Raw pain with no letup. Sickness in the stomach. And a cascade of sobbing tears.

You and I may pride ourselves on being strong and confident, less susceptible to certain swings of emotion than others are. But not at moments like these. Not usually. At that crucible instant, under that many pounds of life-altering weight, each of us is past the mortal limit of our coping equipment. We stumble. We fall. We wail. We are momentarily beyond all comfort.

What happens next, of course, is different for different people. I can only describe what it was like and has been like for me. But I do feel it's important for us to try talking it out, sharing how we've experienced these things.

In grief we become like travelers who have been to a distant country, coming back to meet others who are soon to go or will one day go there. In one way or another, everyone we know will make this painful trip. And God has given us firsthand reports to tell us what it's like. No, we may not be able to dampen the actual effects of grief for others, even in our best attempts at portraying it, but we can at least take some of the mystery out of it. They can look into our eyes, take our hand, and see that we've survived, that this can be endured. By the hardest.

To others—to those who, like us, have already been to this dreadful place—it helps them to be able to sit across the table and relate with someone who knows, who understands. This can be comforting to them in some measure. And I hope that in following me through my own odyssey of grief, now going on four years, that the common threads of our experience, where they appear, will help you move through your own grieving process with new clarity. I'm sure there are others within your sphere of friendship or personal interaction who could benefit from hearing what *you* have found your grief to be like.

For me, in the days and weeks that followed Melissa's death, I experienced several discernable emotions and sensations. One is what I would call *fog*, which I found to be extremely disorienting. A gauze of distance and blurriness seemed to separate me from the reality existing around me. My level of awareness of the outside world seemed almost deadened or weakened, as though I'd experienced a sudden voltage drop that affected some sensory part of my brain.

And yet in another way, this fog seems (to me) a protective gift from God. If one were able to completely feel what their heart had just experienced, without being able to cushion it against the thick padding of this cocooning mist, the load would perhaps be physically unbearable. I fear so. This fog, if that's the best word for it, does seem to possess some pain-reducing qualities.

In fact, I believe this particular filter of grief is what provided me the needed strength to preach my scheduled sermon on the Sunday following Melissa's funeral. It wasn't because I was strong; it was because I was still in shock. I just wasn't feeling much. I was experiencing what I believe to be a God-given defense mechanism I've heard others describe as well: a fog or haziness that somehow blocks much of our sentient awareness.

Perhaps you can attest to what I'm describing. Perhaps it's how you, like me, were able to keep going through some of those hardest, first days. It's a very real effect. Haunting, blanketing—like frost on a gray, chilly morning—and yet a blessed protection from becoming completely consumed in the dark, hollow chamber of hurt and pain.

A second lingering, related feeling I experienced was a sense of *lostness*. Distinct from the dampening effect of fog, this impression contained more of the elements of disbelief than mere disorientation. I found myself occasionally having to shake my mind free from the notion that this earth-shattering event didn't actually happen. It's the way you might feel when resurfacing from sleep or from a dream. You can be walking or driving down a familiar street, seeing things situated as you've always known them to be, and for a brief moment you don't know exactly where you are emotionally. You think this common, everyday scene shouldn't be here because your *loved one* isn't here. For you the whole world has turned upside down. Then why is everybody else just going about their business as though nothing's happened? Don't they realize this is not the same place it used to be? Where am I?

Fog. Feeling lost. Those are two examples of grief's possible incarnations. Some people also report feeling a deep wrenching of *anger*, either at God or at the individual himself or herself, or both, although this anger can actually create a target of anyone—anyone who might be perceived as shouldering blame for what happened. I've certainly had moments when my grief was tinged with anger at this needless loss.

Others describe an eddying tidal pool of *regret*. They feel thrashed about by one round of tormenting conjecture after another: if only they'd been there, if they'd done something differently, if they hadn't lost their temper, if they hadn't been so impatient, if they'd followed up on their first suspicions and inclinations, if they'd turned right instead of left, if they'd have made one more attempt at reconciliation, if they'd have known better what to say when this person was more open to listening. *If. If. If.* I don't know that any of us escapes our heavy periods of grief, particularly the grief that follows a suicide, without at least occasionally feeling the miserable, agonizing undertow of remorse.

But if I had to choose one emotional experience that overshadowed them all for me, it would be this: the preponderance of what I would call *waves*—waves of grief—steady and yet at times unexpected. They rise, they crest, they crash, they enforce their full weight and pressure, then they slowly recede, only to cycle back through their pulsating rhythms again and again.

I can't say I'm out from under the shadow of these waves even now. I don't know that I'll ever be. At any random point of the day, I'm either directly underneath their fury, or I'm catching my breath from the last one, resting in an uneasy peace, awaiting the next assault. Not all of them land with capsizing strength anymore; some only rock me slightly backward without significantly affecting or upsetting my balance. But I feel them. I sense them. And if I didn't have God and His Word to help me, the steadying comfort of His Spirit, the love of family, daily work that requires complex thought and constant interaction with others, I would hate to imagine what these waves of grief could do to me.

Thank God He holds them back for needed periods of time. I would never wish to stand in their path without trusting His shielding hand.

After the first year—the first spring, the first summer, the first passing of her birthday, the first Christmas, which fell only shortly after her death—I found that most of the protective fog and the perplexing sense of lostness had eased. Not until making the turn into that second year—the second year without hearing her voice or seeing her face—did my personal grief seem to crystallize into this one, now familiar, yet increasingly withering battle with the waves of sorrow.

I don't know about you, if you're as far along into your time line as we are, but the second year after Melissa's passing was unexpectedly much harder than the first. I suppose the second time through the calendar, realizing you've now lived every combination of month and date in this new, uncharted, and redefined world of yours, your mind somehow finally gets the full picture that this—*this!*—is your new normal. Despite your grief and the grueling emotions of each day, the world really *has* gone on without her. You *knew* that, but now you *feel* that. In a deeper, surer, sadder way.

In my experience this just brought on more waves.

People told me these waves would decrease over time in both frequency and intensity. And they have. But this was not my experience throughout the balance of that second year. Only in the days since, throughout the third year, heading into the fourth, have I noticed them easing and becoming more manageable. Her birthdays are still hard. Shockingly hard at times. The lilt of a certain song, the sight of a little blonde toddler skipping along beside her father in a parking lot, a passing comment or television commercial, the scent of her favorite perfume wafting through a church lobby or department store—any little thing can bring on the cold, salty grip of another wave.

I wish I could stop them and wash them away, not only for me but for you. I wish I could devise a healing program that promised you could wake up one morning, and these surges of grief would just be gone, never to return.

I can't. They don't.

But as deeply as they hurt, the comfort of the Lord goes deeper still. As unexpectedly as they can surface, God's faithful ever-presence denies them the lethal element of complete surprise. He is the difference. He is survival. "Acquainted with grief" (Isa. 53:3 KJV), He is able to support us in ours. Truly, to be without Him is the only situation our grief cannot endure.

A Theology of Grief

The grief following suicide is so raw and real, so primal and human, even people of faith must often battle just to ride it out, to render it livable. We are not so spiritually untouchable that the physical, emotional pain cannot overwhelm us at times.

But as the days go by and the waves pass in and out and through, our understanding of God—our theology of grief, if you will—exerts a continual impact on how we endure our suffering. Yes, each of us must still bear up under the load. It doesn't necessarily become easier or lighter simply because we can see it even dimly through the eyes of God's greater perspective. But the counsel of Scripture does secure us with the stabilizing beam of truth.

How one grieves depends on what one believes.

And for me, it all starts with a single word. A word that transforms grief from endless to at least endurable. A word that distinguishes Christian faith from all other forms of religious thought and practice. A word that can descend beneath the deepest, darkest cavity of hurt and sorrow you can ever experience. Your pain cannot dig anywhere this word cannot go. Even if you have recently been knocked off balance by the most disrupting shovelful of anguish yet, one that has dropped your emotional footing from a depth that was already so low you thought it couldn't possibly go any lower—still, even at the bottom of that, lives the one word that changes everything.

That word is *hope*.

Hope is a regular participant in Scripture. But because of the honest, true-to-life nature of the Bible, many of the dozens of instances where *hope* is mentioned come from people who, like some of us, were crying out in lonesome despair, wondering (and doubting) if any hope was left. The grieving, embittered Naomi comes to mind. The woeful, inconsolable Job. The persecuted prophets of old, overtasked with proclaiming their ruggedly difficult truths. And yet weaving through every story, for as long as God's work on earth has been told and written down, runs the seamless river of His abiding hope.

"I will put my hope in You, LORD. . . . I will put my hope in Your name . . . the hope of all the ends of the earth and of the distant seas" (Ps. 38:15; 52:9; 65:5). "I thought: My future is lost, as well as my hope from the LORD. . . . My affliction and my homelessness, the wormwood and the poison. I continually remember them and have become depressed. Yet I call this to mind, and therefore I have hope: Because of the LORD's faithful love, we do not perish, for His mercies never end. They are new every morning; great is Your faithfulness! I say: The LORD is my portion, therefore I will put my hope in Him" (Lam. 3:18–24).

When hope enters the picture, arid deserts turn into fountains of oasis. Parched land moistens and cools. Bottomless springs release their thirst-quenching waters. Death, appearing to have prevailed and conquered, meets up with the one thing it cannot kill.

Hope.

The apostle Paul ministered among a pagan world that offered no theological placeholder for life after death. A noteworthy grave inscription from that time period articulates their belief well: "I was not / I became / I am not / I care not." Socrates and a handful of other philosophers tried to cobble together a plausible case for hopeful, eternal happiness, but the man on the street in first-century Greece could not rest his head at night on any assurance. All was leading to nothingness, to emptiness. And for the fledgling believers in the bustling, commercial city of Thessalonica, who were redeemed from unbelief yet worried that their departed loved ones might be unaccounted for at the return of Christ, Paul delivered some comforting news from the Spirit of God Himself: "We do not want you to be uninformed, brothers, concerning those who are asleep, so that you will not grieve like the rest, who *have no hope*" (1 Thess. 4:13, emphasis added).

The believer in Christ who dies is safe in the arms of Jesus and will come back in joyful celebration with Him when He returns to gather His church for all eternity (vv. 14–17). Count on it. Scripture is clear that those in Christ, as soon as they are "out of the body," are "at home with the Lord" (2 Cor. 5:8). There is hope.

Likewise, we who survive in the meantime can be confident that our "hope will not disappoint us" as we cling to Him for comfort and rescue (Rom. 5:5). That's why Paul could say to the Thessalonian faithful, after declaring to them the resolute power of hope: "Therefore encourage one another with these words" (1 Thess. 4:18).

Because hope will carry us through.

Hope tells us that God is still active and working in the lives of His people. Hope reminds us that even when all appears to be invisible silence from heaven, our God is still very real, still highly engaged, still moving quite capably and compassionately behind the scenes. Hope is what opens our eyes and ears to receive in full the loving expressions of our friends, the uplifting counsel of our various support systems, and even those unplanned moments when the Lord sends across our paths what the Bible calls "angels unawares" (Heb. 13:2 KJV)—touches of God that communicate His nearness and knowledge of us in the most unlikely of settings.

We grieve. Oh, how we grieve. But not without hope.

And not without another great Bible word—*hesed*—an ancient Hebrew term that's actually untranslatable into English. Perhaps this obscure fact alone tells us something of its weighty, incomparable nature. Pronounced *HEH-sed* (emphasis on the first syllable), this word is sometimes translated in Old Testament Scripture as "faithful love," sometimes "kindness," sometimes "loyalty," sometimes "mercy." It is the covenant love of God, driven immovably into the ground, unshakable, unchangeable, unending—unbelievable. It is an expression of God's intimate feeling toward us, the way He faithfully reaches out to us. It tells us He is not only acquainted with our hearts to the very back wall and subflooring, but He is also unwilling to be called away on other business while He tends to our need. Not now. Not ever.

The throb of grief, don't we know, is deeper than anyone can reach, even those who love us the best and hurt for us the most. It's like an itch we can't scratch, a wound we can't treat, a problem we can't solve. It requires the unique suture and skillful hand of the One who actually knit this heart of ours together in the first place, the One who knew even those long years ago that we would need to be built to sustain such a devastating loss. And being the only One with a strong enough flashlight, a deep enough probe, and a warm enough compress to stop the swelling, He faithfully, loyally, kindly, mercifully—*covenantally*—plunges into our aching grief. And He never stops absorbing the part of our pain we could never endure without Him.

My middle daughter, Laura, has told me that at times, when experiencing such a loving touch from the Lord like this, she has felt surprisingly overwhelmed, undeserving really of such knowing attention from God to her need. So personal is He. So compassionate. He has showed her a side of His mercy she had never seen or felt before at such up-close range. Millions—billions—of hurting people in the world, and yet, praise His name, her God would deign to come to her, as though looking her right in the face, saying, "I know where you are, dear, and I know where Melissa is too. I not only have *her*, but I have you as well."

My youngest daughter, Allison, speaks also to the faithful aspect of God's *hesed* in shepherding her through her grief. Not only has He comforted her in places where she was very aware of needing His provision but also in places where she wasn't aware. For instance, even though she often still dreams of Melissa—as most do after the death of someone dear—God has faithfully guarded any of these scattered imaginations of hers from darkening into nightmare. Whenever her sleep is accompanied by one of these shadowy scenes and glimpses of our family, Melissa is simply there—like she would be, like she should be. Who else but the Lord could know my little Allison so well, oversee the stage where her dreams play out at night, and refuse to accept even one upsetting script to be performed there?

Our faithful God. Our merciful God. Our God of all hope and comfort.

He is larger than our grief. Deeper than our pain. When we place our trust in Him, He gives us back a resiliency known only to those who have received by His grace the promise of life eternal. "We have put our hope in the living God," Paul said (1 Tim. 4:10), and "according to His great mercy, He has given us a new birth into a living hope through the resurrection of Jesus Christ from the dead" (1 Pet. 1:3).

The way we grieve truly does depend on what we believe.

Recovering in Waves

I knew what I was interrupting that day by calling Laura to tell her what had happened to her sister. This tragic loss, easily the worst day of her life, would forever share a calendar date with what had once been among the most *exciting* days of her life: the birthday of her firstborn son. He was fresh in the middle of turning three the morning we all turned a chilling new page in our family's history.

I knew that Allison, too, was in a vulnerable position— away from home, traveling with her husband in Texas to spend Thanksgiving with his family. She was in the car with her in- laws, heading to one set of grandparents for a holiday meal, when my call rang through. All I remember saying was, "She's gone," before losing the ability to say much else or provide any real detail. Knowing the grief I was causing her on the other end of the line, on top of what I was already feeling—I never thought I could experience such fatherly anguish.

The waves were so high that day. Relentless. Hammering. The fog so thick. The pain so deep.

And ever since—and evermore—our lives have been and will always be accompanied by grief. I realize that.

But that doesn't mean grief wins. Just because it's here and hanging around doesn't mean our God has forsaken us. In fact, it means quite the opposite. It means that when I feel the "ropes of death" wrapped around me, the "torrents of destruction" terrifying me, I get to see something in real life I had once only read and marveled at—my God parting the heavens to come down, take hold of me, and pull me "out of deep waters" (Ps. 18:4, 9, 16). I can now join the psalmist in saying that those waves which are "too strong for me," confronting me "in the day of my distress," have not kept the Lord from rescuing and supporting me, bringing me out to a spacious place of new trust and confidence in Him (vv. 17–19).

Like you, I have known the wilderness, the darkness, the gloom, the broken spirit, the desperate desire to reach a place where my mind and body could live again (Ps. 107:4–22). I have been like those who "went to the sea in ships" and found themselves on the dashing waves of a storm-tossed sea, "rising up to the sky, sinking down to the depths, their courage melting away in anguish" (vv. 23, 26). But also like them I have cried out to the Lord in my grief, and He has responded by guiding me safely to harbor. And though for me—for us—the waves may not have quieted to a steady, gentle murmur or returned forever to the peaceful lapping of ankle-deep splashes on the seashore, we can still feel safe within His love and protection, even on days when the storm tide returns (vv. 28–30).

If we're waiting for the complete withdrawal of grief's presence before we can feel whole and useful and able to function capably in life, we will be waiting until Jesus comes. The cessation of the waves is not a realistic expectation. But the presence of His hope and His faithful love is.

So let the waves come. And let us exalt Him. Let us feel our grief. All of it. And let us praise Him even in our suffering. "Let whoever is wise pay attention to these things and consider the LORD's acts of *[hesed]* . . . faithful love" (v. 43, emphasis added).

He's got us. And grief cannot hold us forever.

> *Grief is better than laughter,*
> *for when a face is sad, a heart may be glad.*
> ECCLESIASTES 7:3

A Letter to You

if you're contemplating suicide

Many things come to mind in wanting to speak with you about our sadness over losing Melissa. If you've read any of my remembrances in this chapter at all, I'm sure you've ascertained the depths we traveled through those dark, foggy, unending days.

But pain is pain. And even though we felt it so acutely as the result of our daughter's death, I know you undoubtedly carry a great deal of pain yourself on many days when life is heavy and long, depending on the situation that makes it feel that way for you.

Maybe you haven't lost a child, as we did, but you've certainly felt the loss of *something*—a parent's approval, a marriage bond, a job, a secure outlook—and the suffering you experience is significant indeed. To compare who or what hurts worse, or to be told you shouldn't be as upset as you are, certainly doesn't lessen your own stress and misery. This is no time for telling you to "look on the bright side" or be glad you don't have it as badly as somebody else.

But you and I—whatever the different sources of our pain—do have the same life preservers to cling to. When I speak of them, I'm aware they may not feel very persuasive or helpful at the moment. More like wishful thinking. They don't change the fact that the first-of-the-month bills are coming due or that your life contains the very same circumstances this morning as were there when you went to bed last night.

But what depression sees and what's really happening are not usually the same thing. Our hearts, when they're not lying to us, are demanding that we avoid looking beyond the immediate radius of this week or this weekend. Depression wants us to base all our conclusions—even our concluding arguments for suicide—on these current readings and nothing else.

And yet each of us exists because of a God whose "works have been finished since the foundation of the world" (Heb. 4:3), who set the elements of creation in place through "an order that will never pass away" (Ps. 148:6), who practically holds the trademark on the words "forever and ever." We are dealing with One who isn't bound by what's going on between now and two days from now. "With the Lord one day is like a thousand years, and a thousand years like one day" (2 Pet. 3:8).

So we don't need to trust what our eyes alone can see. We stand here in a box, surrounded on all sides by *hope*—the hope

He extends to the poor, to the weak, to the unworthy, to all of us. Surrounded by His faithful, covenant *love*—behind-the-scenes acts of mercy and grace and protection and deliverance. We can't see them all because we're only human, bound by five senses and twenty-four-hour days. But trust me, they are what's keeping us afloat. If we could understand how He does it, He wouldn't be big enough to trust.

The long history of mankind proves that He alone remains standing when all else has crumbled away. The bleakness of Friday becomes resurrection morn. Even the "faithful witness" of the moon in the sky each night (Ps. 89:37) reminds us just how constant He is.

I urge you not to limit yourself to what hurts and how to fix it. Trust His hope. Trust His love. Keep your thoughts informed by the Word of God, not the worries of this afternoon. There will always be plenty of those, but there will always be more of Him to meet your need.

> *The God of old is your dwelling place, and underneath are the everlasting arms. He drives out the enemy before you and commands, "Destroy!" So Israel dwells securely; Jacob lives untroubled in a land of grain and new wine; even his skies drip with dew. How happy you are, Israel! Who is like you, a people saved by the LORD? He is the shield that protects you, the sword you boast in. Your enemies will cringe before you, and you will tread on their backs.*
> DEUTERONOMY 33:27–29

CHAPTER 7

Prepare for Impact

*A*s much time as I spend in airports, riding beside perfect strangers from one city to the next, meeting people on the ground at churches and seminaries and various gatherings around the country and the world, I don't how many times a month I'm asked the usual get-acquainted questions. Nearly every day.

"Where are you from? What do you do? Have a family?"

"Yes."

"Any children?"

That's the one that always stops me.

"Yes—we have three grown daughters."

"Oh yeah? Where all do they live? Nearby you?"

"Well, one lives in South Carolina, one lives in Oklahoma, and, uh . . . one lives in heaven."

That's about as close as I've been able to come to a satis-factory answer—which seems OK because the people who ask, innocently enough, don't usually have a good comeback either. They show all the signs of wishing they'd kept their mouth shut with a hello, nice to meet you. Some decide they'll go back to reading their in-flight magazine, while some do continue to probe further, usually from a sincere mix of politeness and com-passion, others (though not many) with a little less sensitivity.

But from my experience this everyday interchange repre-sents one of the more practical examples of how Melissa's death continues to impact each of us personally. I'm sure you can entirely relate or could vary the details only slightly to custom-ize my illustration to your own circumstance. I never thought such a simple, straightforward question could floor me. But it does. I feel it every time.

All of us do. Whenever my wife prepares to go into a set-ting where she knows she'll be meeting new people for the first time, she can feel herself bracing for it beforehand. "Tell us a little about yourself," they might say, one of those go-around-the-circle introductions, "just something about your family, your children, things like that." So it's often part of what's on her mind as she's applying the last of her makeup, slipping her coat from the hanger, driving over to the location, getting out of the car. Deep breath. Brave face. *Am I ready for this? I think so. I hope so.*

The question.

Each of my daughters can attest to a similar experience. They've seen how this casual line of inquiry can turn a light conversation into an awkward interplay of silence and sympathy.

So they do what they can to avoid it, trying hard to keep the "small" in small talk. Because even in knowing the question is coming, seeing it rounding the corner and heading straight for them, they never know which of their emotions will show up to greet it. Steadiness and strength? A trembling lip? Unannounced tears? Their guess is as good as mine. You cannot anticipate how you'll react at a given moment, can you?

The only thing I know for sure is this: I know what one of my answers is *not* going to be. Because I gave it once. And I'll never give it again.

I was not yet in good form or practice on how to handle this simple request for personal information, given what had only recently occurred and how it had altered the framework of our lives. The situation I was in that day, I consoled myself later, was one that didn't lend itself to further explanation. There were reasons why I felt it best to do what I did at the time. Part caution, part convenience. But rather than producing the customary answer I'd given for twenty-plus years—"Yes, three daughters"—these familiar words of response hung up momentarily in the wheels of our new family arithmetic, and they came out like this:

"Yes, I have *two* daughters."

If any one moment of my life can rival, for sheer intensity of grief, the one when I first found out Melissa was dead, this singular moment is oddly a close second. I guess it was better than a half-truth; it was a two-thirds truth. And it wasn't meant to be evasive, just avoidant of unnecessary discomfort and distraction, as much for other people's benefit as for mine. But hearing it voiced from my own mouth—"I have two daughters"—recoiled with such a snap of betrayal, I could barely contain a gasp after feeling its sting. I don't know what my expression and demeanor *looked* like to others; I only know what it *felt* like to me. And as soon as I was by myself again, able to assess the internal damage, I promised aloud to Melissa that I would never—*never!*—repeat that mistake.

I have *three* daughters!

I *still* have three daughters!

Not even suicide can take a child away from me . . . and certainly not some randomly formal introduction.

But don't we all know how even this oh-so-common experience—the surface-level banter surrounding a handshake, a hallway, or a Sunday school visitor—can keep the impact of a loved one's death locked into the everyday fiber of life? And so, as you and I continue to work our way through the aftermath of this tragedy, part of our restoration plan involves recognizing where these flash points are, the relationships they threaten, and the opportunities they present us for growth, renewed godliness, and the courageous recovery of our daily lives.

Marital Strain

One of the great challenges of writing a book like this is not knowing exactly who you're speaking to. The reasons that drew you here could vary widely from the reasons that attracted someone else. The loss you've suffered, for example, may not be one of your children, as ours was. In fact, you may have come here only because you're worried about someone who's *currently* suicidal. You're just looking for anything you can think of to prevent it. The loss hasn't happened yet, and you're praying it won't.

But whenever suicide (or even its deadly potential) invades the lives of those who love or who loved this person, the marriages of those within closest proximity will always feel the shock wave—parents and siblings especially. To lose a son or daughter, a brother or sister, means that a surviving marriage must accept into its lifeblood a lifelong sorrow. This harrowing subject or its heavy silences are sure to occasionally occupy a full dinner hour, cut short an evening, dampen a mood, interrupt a holiday celebration. It will often require more patience and understanding than either spouse believes themselves capable of dredging up. And because the *personal* grief we feel in dealing with this painful death can be so daunting all by itself, a wife or husband can often fail to pick up on the struggles of their other partner or simply not possess enough energy in reserve to worry about what's happening to their marriage, only to themselves.

Marriage is a key impact point.

Two things I've noticed, however, tend to cause the most ongoing friction in marriage relationships after they've been forced to accommodate suicide into their vocabulary. One is blame; the other, misunderstanding.

Blame. I'm mostly speaking to parents when I say this (I think), although it could certainly apply to other situations. But because suicide leaves behind so many frayed edges, critical moments, frozen memories, and other bits of unfinished business—loose wires still sparking from the shock, white-hot emotions we can't seem to cool to a safe temperature—we sometimes look elsewhere to try resolving the unresolvable.

Why did you . . . ?
Why didn't you . . . ?
If only you would've . . .
I'll never forgive you for not . . .

Surrounding any suicide are enough what-ifs and wishes that a person could paper the whole house with them, just with the ones he or she alone feels responsible for. Add to these the failures of the other person—whether fairly or unfairly perceived—and you could never run out of regrets and accusations to fling against the walls, headboards, and tabletops as long as you live.

And yet for some couples, instead of realizing the endless futility of this exercise, the practice of blaming becomes the desperate method of choice for venting their grief and anger. It serves as their go-to response. As long as there's a place besides themselves to pin the fault for what happened and what led up to it, they'll run to that blaming spot whenever the crush of grief and resentment is more than they can bear by themselves.

And because a wife or husband is typically the closest target, not to mention usually the simplest one to build a case against, why look anywhere else to pound an argument? To level charges? To demand an apology, even though it would probably never be received as genuinely sufficient? Yes, blaming is usually an end in itself. It's not really asking for anything . . . except for the other person to sit there and take it.

But, of course, many wives and husbands—whether on the giving end or the receiving end—choose not to sit there forever. Marriages are frequently the next in line to die after suicide has claimed its initial victim.

So in dealing with the impact of tragic death on a marriage, one of the first action items must be to resolve *not* to do something: not to start blaming. Because if you give blame enough room and volume, one house can hardly hold it all in.

A second observation on the impact of suicide in marriage involves the emergence of possible *misunderstanding*. And by this I specifically mean the need for ongoing patience in letting your wife or husband grieve this dreaded loss in his or her own way—whether you understand their way or not. Most often you won't.

At some point after Melissa's death, for example, my wife and daughters went over to her house, with her husband's permission, to take some of the clothes out of her closet. And started to wear them.

Well, I didn't like it. I don't know *why* I didn't like it exactly. I guess I just struggled with seeing the other girls in my life walking around in coats and scarves I remembered seeing Melissa wearing. Beyond that, I just couldn't understand how the feel of her clothes on their skin and shoulders could do anything but shroud them in sorrow, making them miss her all the more. If I were in their shoes, that's certainly the way it would seem to me.

And yet to Dayle and my daughters, putting on these items was like wrapping Melissa around themselves like a blanket. She wasn't there, but she was *there* . . . somehow alive again in cotton, color, and some of her favorite dress patterns. To touch the fabric, to push the sleeves up their arms, to lightly dust their fingertips across the collars and fronts as they preened themselves in the mirror was like being with her all over again, remembering the good times. It didn't necessarily make them *happy*, but it helped them. They needed this.

So my job as a husband was just to let Dayle do it. Without commentary. If wearing Melissa's things provided a desirable outlet for her own grief, why should I forbid her the experience or cripple it with my criticism? It's not the way *I'd* choose to do it, but it made sense and brought comfort to *her*.

We all grieve differently.

And that needs to be OK with us.

Encapsulated within our different grieving responses are all kinds of factors: some of them quite natural according to our basic temperaments; some conditionally developed as a result of past experiences; others admittedly not as healthy as they should probably be, and yet a part of our emotional makeup all the same.

Me—I'm a pretty tenderhearted person, and I do weep sometimes. But often I grieve best by not speaking about troubling things. Analyze this pattern all you like, but I frequently manage my grief better with quiet or sometimes by focusing my attention on other matters.

It's not because I'm trying to forget Melissa. Not at all. I'm not meaning to escape or deny. The truth is, she is almost *always* on my mind. I daresay not a single hour goes by, day or night, that I don't think of her. And yet if I were being expected or compelled to talk constantly about what I'm feeling or thinking in regard to her, it would tend to complicate and intensify my grieving, more than I could bear. I love thinking about Melissa, remembering her laughter and her bubbly nature, seeing her thin, little hands raised in worship with her head thrown back, singing with all her heart. But how thankful I am to the Lord for my sweet wife, who so often gives me the freedom *not* to talk about my grief at those moments when I'd simply rather refrain.

Some, however, do need to talk it out. Some need to cry. Others, on the other hand, may *not* want to cry—and not because they're insufficiently sorrowful. Some will want other people around to console them, to commiserate with them. Others will need their isolation, at least for a little while. Some are comforted by pictures, videos, and recordings of their loved one. Others just aren't ready to sit down with those things yet.

These are not rights and wrongs, areas in which any of us should be judged or condemned. This is simply how our individual hearts, minds, and bodies react to heavy sadness. And because a suicide is likely the heaviest sadness you've ever experienced in your life to date, you may be surprised even yourself at how it's affecting you and what it's exposing about your nature. How much less do you need someone else disparaging you for this, not approving of the way you're coping, attacking you in your most vulnerable state?

If ever you needed *each other*, it's now. Just to hold on together. To trust God valiantly as a couple. To cry in each other's arms. To respect your differences. To realize you're stronger as a unit, even with your shared weaknesses and disappointments. Anything that divides you is sure only to add to your longtime sorrow.

Marriage is a secondary, collateral target of nearly every suicide. Know that. Expect that. And realize that your marriage is now more dependent than ever on your willingness to forgive, to avoid blame and argument, and to allow one another to be yourselves, particularly through those first months and years following a tragic event, when emotions and sensitivities are still so painful to the touch.

No one is ready for this. *No one.* But we can stay resolved to preserving what remains, including the oft-undervalued treasure of each other. We're much harder to carry off when we're hanging on together.

Family Issues

Parenting is always a delicate balance, being careful not to overlook what any of our children need while we're busy handling everything else life demands of us. Dayle and I endeavored as best we could to be extremely fair and equal with each child at every stage of our family's life, which frequently proved difficult because of the amount of focused time and energy Melissa often required of us. Our daughters truly loved one another and enjoyed being together, but some of Melissa's outbursts and unpredictabilities did create wedges in their relationship, straining at their loyalties and adding a level of discomfort and distance among them.

Her death, therefore, even though it occurred after both of our other daughters were grown and married, reignited their memories of certain tensions and left behind some emotional baggage to sort through and try folding into their futures.

Laura, for example—slightly more than two years younger than Melissa—had instinctively taken on more of a big sister role as they grew through their teenage years, feeling more and more responsible for saving Melissa from herself each time she'd veer into the traffic of oncoming danger.

Allison, our youngest, never one to seek attention or the spotlight, had grown sometimes embarrassed by the situations Melissa was capable of getting her into. Melissa's personality was one that felt energized if she was being noticed or making a scene, but Allison—reserved, mature, unassuming—felt distressed whenever made the center of unwanted attention. As a result, she was left with little choice but to shy away from Melissa to some degree. This caused difficulty for Allison, as she was the one closest geographically to where Melissa lived. Because of constant interaction between the two, the relationship was often strained. Melissa's demands for a close sister relationship were difficult, and she often made it impossible for Allison. Laura, on the other hand, was geographically more than a thousand miles distant. Allison worked hard and prayed hard about how to be a good sister to Melissa, although everyone who was aware of the situation knew it was a very challenging task to accomplish on an ongoing, consistent basis.

If you're a brother or sister to someone who's committed suicide, then you understand what some of my girls' struggles have been like. Laura wasn't there when Melissa died. She was at home with her family, half a country away, where she should have been. And yet, as the person who had always felt most responsible for "saving" her sister, she has had a hard time getting over the fact she wasn't there when Melissa needed saving the most.

Justifiable guilt? Of course not. But painful? Troubling? Used by the enemy to mockingly condemn and deride her? You bet. Every chance he gets.

Not a month before the terrible events of November 27, she had been home for a visit and had seemed to discern that

Melissa was struggling, slipping back. They sat alone in her car one evening while Laura tried desperately to encourage her and remind her of what really mattered in life. But it hadn't been enough. *Why not? Why couldn't I save her? Why wasn't I there? Why did I have to be so far away? I could have done something! I know it!*

Maybe you've felt the same way.

All these questions. All left behind. All unanswered. Because Melissa's not here. And so they'll never know. They'll only wonder and wake up worrying in the night and need more of Jesus than ever before to quiet these taunting voices inside their heads.

What an impact suicide carries.

This is why as parents, even of grown children, we must remember our responsibility to keep shepherding these precious ones. Our pain is bad, obviously, and we could lose ourselves in it without a whimper of resistance. But our children hurt too, and they still need us. Not to be stoic and wooden, shielding our grief from them where they can't see it, afraid that by our being upset we'll only affect them more deeply. Quite the opposite, our openness and honesty before them will give them similar permission to be real with *us* as well, to know they're welcome to shed tears and share memories in our presence.

In many cases these children may already be blessed with the faithful love of a spouse to lean on or the caring companionship of good friends. But they never outgrow their need for a parent's love. A parent's approval. A parent's acceptance and empathy and consolation. Even apology, where warranted.

So guard these tender relationships—parent and child—recognizing they will come under heavy fire during times like these, just like your marriage relationship. The distance can widen. Bitterness can grow. Decay can set in. Blame can be distributed.

Or else you can spot the threat to you and your children and draw them close. Perhaps closer than ever before, or at least closer than you've been for a long time. Not in a way that becomes codependent or unduly challenges their autonomy as an adult, as a wife or husband, as a mother or father, but simply as a means of acknowledging that you're grieved for *their* grief as well. That you care. That you're here. And that you will stand strong and move forward yourself because you want to be strong for *them*. Strong in the Lord. Strong in His Word. Teaching by example that His supply is truly unlimited, inexhaustible—even in the midst of something this overwhelming.

Marriage and family. The building blocks of society. The cradle and covenant that forms so much of our identity as individuals. Where else would our enemy choose to unload his next assault after weakening our perimeter with the deathblow of suicide? Evil and opportunistic as he is, why wouldn't we expect him to strike quickly where his chances of inflicting additional damage are the greatest?

Knowing your enemy and his strategies doesn't make the battle go away. But it does help you know where to focus the best of your depleted energies, converging them on the places where they can do their most important work: loving the most important people in your life.

Ingrown Grief

Suicide's impact, of course, may often start close to home, as we've seen. But it can keep spreading out into other circles of relationship and influence, threatening our healthy interaction with the outside world.

Most all of us can attest to grief's felonious desire to kidnap and drag us into the shadows of seclusion. But as surely as it seeks to take us off by ourselves, to make us feel strangely secure inside our prisons of solitary confinement, we must each bear personal responsibility for plotting an escape. For breaking free. For working our way out.

I say this, dear friend, with the most tender sensitivity because I understand, especially if you find yourself in the early stages of grief, that all you may feel capable of doing right now is just getting up in the morning, performing the bare minimum of daily life functions, and then going wearily, woefully back to bed as soon as possible. Many of us who share the pain of our particular situation can relate to the gnawing presence of this downward tug.

And even though, as mentioned earlier, your temperament of grief may naturally be more the type that makes you need to sit alone, lights out, shutting down for at least certain stretches of time, shunning most all forms and faces of human contact, I only want to jump in here long enough to encourage this light, caring, friend-to-friend warning:

Please don't let this tendency petrify into a lifestyle.

One of Satan's tactics is to pull us inward and not let us go. To lead us into becoming very self-focused and withdrawn. And as with the other impacts of suicide on our marriage and family, we need to be able to recognize this and be aware it's going on. No one who is truly concerned for our overall welfare would stand by and not tell us whenever we are reaching danger points of introversion. I surely don't want it to happen to you.

I'm thinking of a woman who called me recently, engulfed under heaving waves of depression and despair. "I'm not going to commit suicide," she said, "I feel sure of that. But it's all I can think about." The introversion had fastened itself so rigidly onto her heart that it was drawing her toward the only conclusion to which such thinking can lead—*checking out*—if not terminally, at least mentally and emotionally and certainly spiritually.

Life, as hard as it is—indescribably more difficult, of course, once a tragedy like ours has struck—is simply more than one person can handle alone. So when we and our own thoughts become about the only resistance we employ against our various foes and fears, we naturally lose the grip on our ability to handle things. "I've just got to take care of *me*," I hear people say. "Nobody will do it if I don't." But the problem is, *we* are never enough by ourselves. And so introversion becomes a bit of a curse, a self-defeating principle, if we ever allow it to dominate and sink us.

Certain elements of our grief, perhaps much of it, will follow us all the way to our graves. That's just reality. But we do need to be mindful and honest when we feel the grief getting away from us, taking us over, burying us in isolation from friends and church and other meaningful relationships, crippling our ability to function long-term.

Some of you, hopefully reminded again of God's faithful love as you've been reading this book, have felt a rise of divine strength issuing up from deep within you. He's buoying you out of the depths, at least in slow steps and stages, back where you can see light and color, where you can feel the wind of healing on your face and in the air. But others—though every ounce a believer in Christ—are simply not finding this to be your life experience. The promises of God that once flowed so freely and seemed so watertight: you still *believe* them (most days), but you're just not *seeing* them right now. And it's making you want to run and hide—away from *Him*, away from everybody.

I've talked with friends whose grief is still so fresh, so exposed at the surface, so apt to produce uncontrollable tears at almost every remembrance, it's currently keeping them from living. They simply have not been able to scramble back to their feet, long after their initial loss. They've backed away from help and the perceived intrusion of others' love. They don't know how else to get through this but to wall the world off. All they feel is hurt. This grief is just too much. Even still.

And I understand that. You don't have to fake it with me. But if I could offer you just two bits of firsthand advice, here's what I'd say:

First, *begin inching out of the cocoon of introversion.* If you know you've been drawing inward, lacking strength to cope with others' looks and the everyday jostle of life, select at least one simple excursion soon that will take you gently out of yourself. Ask a friend to a quiet lunch. Invite one of your closest couples over to the house for coffee. Begin reentry into your Sunday school class or some other group experience you've stopped attending. Shop for a birthday present. Write a thank-you note. By turning your face even slightly toward an outward exposure, you'll begin sensing a warmth that can slowly but surely bring you out of the cold.

Second, *try not to be afraid of feeling again.* Part of the pull of introversion—not all of it but some—is an attempt at pain avoidance. Which is understandable but also undermining. One way to steadily dampen the blow of suicide's impact, ironically, is to let it come in and do its worst. Not to suppress it. To look it squarely in the eye and see it for what it is.

The hurt means you're alive. It means your body is reacting and willing to fight—both to fight back and fight through it. So rather than running from grief's harsh reality, you may find that in letting it groan and pierce and ache and cry, you begin to exhaust some of its staying power. You expose its secret hiding places. You force it into the open air where it can be more easily outlined and dealt with.

And not only that, but by letting others share it and shoulder it with you—rather than pretending you don't need them or that you're doing just fine—you'll likely feel its merciless grip loosening even more, or at least more often. By holding onto life, your family, your friends, and your God, the muscles you're working as He guides you forward will build endurance that will only strengthen and develop over time.

If you say you're just not there yet—not ready to feel and trust and hope and engage—please don't feel guilt about that. Don't assume defeat because of the time that's passed and the weakness you still feel. But don't quit either. As hard as it may be to believe, there's still a life out there for you. And you're one day nearer to it than you were just yesterday.

Reversal of Roles

Like the waves of grief described in the previous chapter, the impact of suicide contains a relentless, recurring nature. The initial force, never more intense than at the knee-buckling moment of first discovery, still reverberates forward without ever losing its full ability to pound and shiver.

It can be tricky and unpredictable. You may even find, after years of feeling somewhat steady and immune from its most debilitating punches, the pain suddenly surfaces and surprises you out of nowhere. Laura, for example, was deep in the midst of babies and toddlers at the time of Melissa's death. There was no slowing down her life, no matter what her emotions were calling and crying for. But after her young children had grown beyond their more helpless, needy stages, when a mother's time is not quite as consumed with diapers and feedings and trips to the drug store for pink medicine, she began to notice an intensity of grief she had previously stuffed underneath her busy schedule. Now it was emerging from its holding bin. Still potent and imposing. No less jagged and biting. Able to press down and disrupt.

So we can't outrun it entirely. The impact of suicide lingers on. But the fruit of God's Spirit is still able to grow, even in places without sun or water or many of the other conditions we typically consider necessary for spiritual strength and cultivation. Abiding in Him, we can still produce love, patience, and self-control at home, blessing our wife or husband with the gift of our grace and understanding. We can still foster a place of peace and kindness, even joy (if you can still imagine such a thing)—key ingredients our children can use in rebuilding and recovering. We can recapture the goodness, faithfulness, and gentleness that are necessary to growing friendships, meaning-ful work, and servant-hearted giving. We can worship. We can trust. We can turn this deadly impact into something much more positive.

Look at us. Comforting others. Touching hearts. Mirroring the immensity of God's help in times of trouble. Turning around this blunt force that's been hurled against us until amaz-ingly, supernaturally, it's actually propelling us forward.

That's how we men and women—survivors of suicide's impact—become people of impact ourselves.

> *You pushed me hard to make me fall,*
> *but the LORD helped me. The LORD is my strength*
> *and my song; He has become my salvation.*
> PSALM 118:13–14

A Letter to You

if you're contemplating suicide

The questions. "How many children do you have?" "How many brothers and sisters?" "Where do they live?" "What do they do?" These questions have no better answers for me than the ones you're asking yourself right now. "What's the point?" "Why is life worth living?" "How am I supposed to handle this?" "Who even cares?"

What I'm saying is, suicide doesn't make the questions go away. It just leaves someone else to answer them. And while we love you enough that we'll go to *any* lengths of personal sacrifice or discomfort if that's what life demands of us, we desperately want to invest our energies exploring answers *with* you rather than fielding them *without* you.

Few if any of these questions—the ones you ask when no one's there to hear you, the ones you may not want anyone to know you're even pondering—can be answered in a tight package or paragraph and then presented to you as indisputable evidence. I know you don't expect to rise up from one simple discussion and rationally dismiss what made you ever ask these things in the first place.

But answers to questions this large and complex must be given the space of days and time to unfold themselves. By scrawling your own punctuation, forcing by suicide to turn the question mark into a period, you close out a sentence that still contains all the potential elements of a good story. You shut the book before it's had a chance to show you where God is going with all this background material. There is still so much to redeem of your past, so many positive things that can arise amid your current difficulties—and the power of Almighty God behind you to make it happen.

The questions we should be asking are ones that leave room for redemptive possibilities, not those that imply negative responses, ones in which we are unwilling to consider hope and patience as workable alternatives. Instead of biting off enormous imponderables that leave us peeling the onions of circular thinking, let's deal with some things that are a bit more manageable, areas that raise the likelihood of success. Simple victories. Steady advances. Fighting chances. The kind that build momentum, turn the playing field, and put you in a stronger, less tentative position for approaching the next challenge.

I don't know anyone who doesn't ask questions or who doesn't believe that the ones they're asking are the only ones that really matter right now. But if you can just keep asking these questions out loud, with people who care and want to help, what you may not find by way of suitable answers will be compensated for in the process of being loved and heard.

As believers in Christ, we don't need to run from the hard stuff. God's Word and His all-wise plans for His people ensure that no questions of ours can come anywhere near the perimeters of His abilities to manage—as if such perimeters existed. I promise you, within this vast expanse of His omnipotent ability is room enough for you and your questions to live at the same time.

So ask them, but please—*please*—don't think you need to die for them. "No" is the only right answer when suicide is the question.

> *Listen to my words, LORD; consider my sighing.*
> *Pay attention to the sound of my cry, my King and my*
> *God, for I pray to You. At daybreak, LORD,*
> *You hear my voice; at daybreak I plead my case*
> *to You and watch expectantly.*
> PSALM 5:1–3

CHAPTER 8

Back to Life

*T*he months following Melissa's death would have been unsettling enough under any circumstances. Had it happened a year earlier, for instance, I would have been senior pastoring, heading into the Advent and Christmas season. I don't know what would have become of my usual preaching and ministry duties as a result, but I would certainly have needed to call on other members of our staff to cover for some of my responsibilities and likely absences. Knowing our deacons, I could imagine their insisting that I take all the time I needed to heal and recover before returning to the pulpit. My heart, heavily broken, would have been torn with concern both for my congregation and for my family.

As it turned out, however—and little did we know in advance—the shock of Melissa's death erupted amid a choice we had already made to "unsettle" ourselves in ministry. We were in the midst of transitioning to Atlanta (as I've previously shared), disrupting our usual routine and structure with rental housing and moving boxes. But no sooner had I begun to adjust into my new role as vice president of evangelism for our North American Mission Board than the opportunity arose to become president and CEO of our denomination's executive committee in Nashville, precipitating another move—two within a matter of months.

In any list of the top five or ten marital stressors, the experiences of "moving" and "death of a family member" always rank high. So while we sensed God's hand and calling in directing us to accept this newest assignment, we also felt the unusual strain of what we were going through. And yet He led us along by His strong right arm, sustaining us with His promised "daily bread," and faithfully rousing the sun in the eastern sky each morning, whether we were ready to receive its bright appearing or not.

Completing the closing process on a new home, learning a new city, and recovering our personal belongings from many months in temporary storage were both relief and tormenting reminder, all at the same time. Every stitch of clothes and stick of furniture carried us back in our minds, each of them bearing almost photographic witness to a life forever altered by the events of the previous November. We never knew how the next puncture of packing tape on the next moving box would affect us, only that we would need to simultaneously cry and carry on, setting up housekeeping by steady degrees, one carton and container at a time.

And I was doing pretty well . . . until I stumbled upon a particularly unexpected surprise.

I had actually forgotten that more than a year before, I had asked Melissa if she would be willing to help me pack up the veritable library of books contained in my office. She was out of work at the time, and I offered to pay her a little money for the hours she invested. It was nice to have her around—it really was—even if she did spend a good bit of time on the phone or texting friends. But in the end we did a lot of laughing and reminiscing together, and she proved an invaluable help in breaking down my study for easy setup on the other end.

Here I was in downtown Nashville then—summer of 2010—beginning the dusty process of knifing into the corrugated cardboard tops, preparing to stock my new, empty shelves with old, heavy books and office mementoes. And there, on the top volume in the very first box I opened, resting at a slant, was a single yellow sticky note.

Written in Melissa's cute, recognizable hand.

And it simply said this: "I love you, Daddy."

Mmmh.

I lost it. Dropping into my chair, my shoulders heaving, I flicked my eyeglasses onto the bare desktop and wept as quietly as I could, spurred on by a kaleidoscope of emotions. Sadness? Oh my, yes. Familiar waves of sadness. And yet somehow the stream of steady tears running down my face contained a distinguishable note of sweetness along with its bitter sting and taste.

Oh, how I missed my little Melissa in that moment! What I wouldn't have given to see her stacking books and papers just off to the side there, the way I'd seen her doing in a similar office setting the last time these boxes and I were together. What I wouldn't have done to hear those tender words—"I love you, Daddy"—coming not merely from the thin blue lines and loops of a common, ordinary stick pen but directly from her pursed, playful lips.

And yet, look at that. That precious note. Truly like a message from the grave.

"I love you, Daddy."

I love you too, Melissa.

And in each box, another: "I'm so proud of you." "Thank you for being there for me no matter what." "It's no mystery why God has chosen you." "You'd better come back and see us as often as possible." One of them even harked back to that silly, little children's song I told you I sang to the girls on the way to school every morning—"You Are My Sunshine!"

I tell you, it was like striking gold.

Or, no, on second thought, striking gold would feel more akin to finding a penny in the parking lot compared to this. What I experienced that special morning, sunlight gleaming through the clean wall of windows, Melissa speaking to me from every single moving box . . .

Priceless.

Today those individual notes are laminated on several letter-size pieces of paper and treasured in a top drawer where I can get to them any moment of the day. I have pulled those pages from my desk, I don't know, *hundreds* of times in the months and years since, just to look at them again. And again. And again. They have helped me get through some difficult days, those little yellow notes.

They have helped me heal.

And, oh, how we all need to heal.

You and I meet in books and places like these for two basic reasons: (1) looking for someone who can relate to our suffering, and (2) looking for answers that can lead us to brighter days.

Looking for healing.

And let me tell you what I find most remarkable about the healing God gives, even for those of us who have borne one of life's most unthinkable hurts. Wonderful and compassionate as He is, God doesn't wait to start our healing at some portion of the journey where we finally hit bottom and can go nowhere else but up. In His great wisdom and even more astonishing love, our Lord planned for our healing many years in advance, sowing seeds of recovery in the dirt and rain and heat and darkness, just waiting to bring them up fresh and green in the spring—ready when we need them, food that anticipates our hunger.

That day in my South Carolina office, for example, when I asked Melissa for help in packing up my books, God was healing me. Already.

I just didn't know I was dying yet.

That's how far in advance He was working to encourage and uplift my sagging heart.

And in ways both large and small, He has already gone ahead of you as well. He has ordered His living mercies, established His eternal plans, and created custom healing opportunities so that you can always be assured of hope as you learn to know Him and depend on Him. It's not an *if* but a *when*. Not a someday but a certainty. Not later. Now.

Expect Him to heal you.

No, not everything we deal with is fun. Not every experience is pleasurable. But we can count on having what we need to sustain us, knowing that it will be enough. And in this final chapter I'd like to give you three distinct categories where this healing most commonly comes from—and wonderfully comes to stay.

Leaning on Jesus

As much as we love God's forgiveness, we'd love to think we didn't need it quite so much—at least not as much as some other people do. No matter how the Bible refutes it, and no matter how our Christian theologies argue against it, we still often live as though we're trying to impress God. We want to do things right. We want to be the model. We want to not think we depend as much on His grace as we actually do.

But when suicide strikes a family, it yanks down the curtain from around such misinformed identities and desires. In that moment our need, though already present, is fully exposed—to us, to everybody. And as deeply as we feel the loss, we also feel a large measure of the fault and blame for what happened. That's why a lot of our inner conversations that take place afterward assume the form of open-ended questions: "What could I have done differently?" "Why didn't I try harder?" Men and women who'd once had hopes of being the perfect parent, the ideal spouse—of being a person who brings only good and blessing into the lives of those they love—can convince themselves following a suicide they've never done *anything* right.

Ultimately, of course, no one else is responsible for another individual's choice to end their life, even though any of us who are close to the situation would admit our own mistakes in handling certain elements of the relationship. But bottom line, we're not perfect. Could *never* have been perfect. And the various choices we made along the way—we made them out of love. They were our best attempts at discipline or fairness or treatment strategies or whatever the pressing situation was calling for.

If we had discerned a few things more accurately, if we had been paying closer attention, we might have made different decisions than we did. No question. But at some point as we begin to deal with it and process it, we must cast our broken hearts on Jesus and simply trust that He understands—that He forgives us where forgiveness is needed, that He knows and knew our personal limitations, and that He loves us throughout every circumstance, past and present.

Dayle and I have in no way been immune from questioning ourselves. Self-doubts and regrets can still ticker-tape across our minds, even today. But on the basis of God's Word, He has led us to accept, "OK, Lord, You did not expect us to be perfect parents. We were never perfect to begin with. And as much as we wanted to fix what Melissa needed fixing, to assist in making her feel whole and complete as a person, You are the only One capable of doing that without error, flaw, or fatigue."

So . . . we let go.

We let go of our guilt.

We sat back and received God's mercy and forgiveness.

It wasn't easy. It never is. And we've needed to keep doing it on repeated occasions, both personally and as a couple. But we have thrown our tired, grief-torn selves onto Jesus. And we have trusted Him as our only hope for moving on.

By letting go, you and I are certainly not overlooking our mistakes, nor are we dismissing the memory of our lost loved one as if they didn't exist by moving on without them. We still want to learn what we can glean from how we handled (or mis-handled) a variety of difficult matters so that we can apply these lessons both to future situations in our own lives and in helping other people from our firsthand experiences. But if we *don't* let go, what we're really saying is that we should have been capable of taking care of these problems without God's help. If we don't let go, what are we really holding on to?

If we're the only ones we'll leave on the hook for this "fail-ure" as a parent, spouse, sibling, or whatever, we're essentially declaring that we knew better than God what was happening and what could have been done to stop it. Our grief is exposing our self-reliant, self-sufficient, self-focused nature. Strange but true because it *feels* like humility and taking ownership. Yet it subtly belies a high trust level in ourselves and a low trust level in God and His sovereign ways.

That's what *anyone* is doing who won't receive God's for-giveness. They're saying they don't need it. Or they're saying they don't feel worthy or good enough for God to love them so outlandishly. But they're still implying that if He knew what they were really like, He wouldn't feel merciful toward them.

Wait a minute. "If He knew?" What makes us think we know ourselves better than He does?

Arrogance in disguise. That's how terribly tricky our enemy is.

So I'm inviting you, my hurting friend, to do what we have been shown to do in Scripture—to place all our doubts, sins, and regrets at the feet of Jesus, recognizing our inability, admitting our great need, and letting His grace do what it was meant to do all along—*forgive us*—despite our prickly, prideful resistance.

Forgive us, Lord!

I know. This is so central to the gospel that we're shocked when such a foundational truth hits us as though we never contemplated such a thing before. But because of who we are on the inside, the precious, pervasive love of God must continually penetrate a thick wall of seductive self-righteousness before it can claim new outposts in our hearts. I pray that in relinquishing yourself from a standard of pure perfection, you will experience His love and provision for your need in a new, healing way.

Looking to Heaven

We walk past a lot of Bible verses reminding us that life is short: "seventy years or, if we are strong, eighty years. Even the best of them are struggle and sorrow; indeed, they pass quickly and we fly away" (Ps. 90:10). Our time here is described as a "breath" (Job 7:7), a "morning mist" (Hosea 13:3), "like smoke that appears for a little while, then vanishes" (James 4:14). Our days are like "dust," like "grass," like a "flower" growing wild in a field. "When the wind passes over it, it vanishes, and its place is no longer known" (Ps. 103:14–16).

So with such brevity of time to spend here, relatively speaking, the Word encourages us to set our minds "on what is above, not on what is on the earth" (Col. 3:2). In heaven is where our lives are actually located if we have believed on Christ's name. We are already "hidden" there, this passage goes on to say, soon to be "revealed with Him in glory" (vv. 3–4).

Therefore we can accurately affirm that "the sufferings of this present time are not worth comparing with the glory that is going to be revealed to us" (Rom. 8:18). "Our momentary light affliction"—which it truly is, hard to believe—"is producing for us an absolutely incomparable eternal weight of glory. So we do not focus on what is seen," the Bible says, "but on what is unseen. For what is seen is temporary, but what is unseen is eternal" (2 Cor. 4:17–18).

Heaven.

Our eyes are to be fixed on heaven.

But they're usually not, are they? Until something like suicide hits. And then people like us can see heaven in a whole new light.

My wife especially inspires me in this, when I consider the healing provided for us through God's unfathomable gift of heaven. During months and years she geared much of her quiet, devotional time to studying what His Word says about heaven— what it's like, what's happening there, how Melissa is experiencing life in this place, how its invisible gleams of hope radiate joy all the way into the darkness of our times and the troubles of our hearts. Dayle's first thoughts of the day, immediately upon rising, are often spent imagining the scenery in heaven that morning.

What are they doing there right this minute?

One of the most heartening, inspiring statements anyone made to her following Melissa's death was something along the lines of, "Every time you go to church and you're worshipping God, remember you're praising Him along with her because Melissa is right there with Him, doing the same thing." We never hear a praise song anymore without knowing we're sharing the experience with our dear, redeemed daughter on the other side. Heaven changes everything.

Suicide, in so many ways, is a dampener. A muter of sounds, smiles, and depth perception. A heavy coat that hangs over our backs, a straitjacket that narrows our field of vision and range of motion. And yet as God would have it, horrific tragedy also disperses many of the complicating distractions that can cloud our view of reality. It strips clean some of the preoccupations, pretensions, and pitiful wastes of time that once seemed so all-important—and still do to the majority of people. Why not use this refined clarity of focus to place our minds and thoughts where Jesus said we should: collecting for ourselves "treasures in heaven" (Matt. 6:20), adding daily to our new discoveries of how the blessings of God are being poured out on our precious loved one and are descending from His throne into our own weary arms?

By looking off to heaven, you and I can actually receive from Him the recovery of our own happiness, knowing this son or daughter, wife or husband, parent or friend—whatever person you've lost in this heartbreaking manner—is happily at rest and enjoying completeness in Christ, assuming that you have confidence in their relationship with Christ.

Darkness will fall on earth again tonight but not where *they* are—and not where we're going. Pain and grief may stop by for a long visit before the day is out, but not where *they* live—and one day not at our door either. Every good, peaceful thing we could ever wish to experience on the other edge of this suicide is already being experienced by the redeemed of the Lord, gathered around His very presence.

Our Melissa is there, and that makes me happy.

It heals me.

Learning to Celebrate

Leaning on Jesus for the freedom that is ours through His grace and forgiveness. *Looking to heaven* for the hope He provides and the place He's prepared, both for us and for our loved one.

And third in this simple, significant list of healing opportunities—the surprise gift of new tools for relearning an old skill.

At one time we didn't need to look far to find something to celebrate. Our threshold for what we deemed excitement worthy was fairly low. An action movie. A bowl game. A good steak, an up-front parking spot, a television series finale. But then life grew harder and more complicated. Nerves and worries crowded into the space that used to be reserved for carefree enjoyments. We could still celebrate exciting things, like a new job opportunity or a new grandchild, but it took a lot more than it did before to keep us up and invigorated.

Then suicide comes. And it comes close to draining whatever

celebration is left in our lives. Pinks and golds look much more like dark rust and brown. Good news falls flat. Special days turn sour. Just about anything that starts out feeling good quickly appears suspect. We see right through it.

But the part of us that once smiled more easily and could feel joy for only minor reasons didn't simply disappear; it just got lost. And once God helps you discover it again, you'll find you're celebrating life with a depth, understanding, and weightiness that makes many of those former delights feel cheap and pointless by comparison. Not only that, but many of the reminders, keepsakes, and visual prompts that link you to your loved one—things that perhaps have remained unbearable for you to hold, handle, or undertake—could in time bring you renewed comfort as God moves you at His gentle pace through the healing process.

As He helps you learn to celebrate again.

I'll admit, I've been slow in opening myself up to this. Maybe you've experienced the same kind of hindrance and hesitation. There are things of Melissa's I haven't been able to hear or see or touch, places I haven't been able to go back to and remember. They still hurt and break me down. They make me want her back so badly, all I can feel sometimes are deep jabs of grief and suffering. But I'm desiring the strength to press forward—not just for me but for her—to steadily grow more adept at *celebrating* her life, not just surviving her loss.

That's what those pages of yellow memo sheets have become for me, by the grace of God. They help me celebrate her heart and spirit. Even though reading them can often make my eyes water, they do increasingly cause my heart to gladden. The Lord knew how much I needed those.

Celebrating Melissa is what writing this book has done— giving me a chance not only to talk about her but to meet *you*, to know God is using her story to help others with whom we share this unenviable situation and partnership. Melissa's death is not dying with her but rather is working to minister to hurting hearts. I can celebrate that.

And we must keep looking for new ways all the time . . . to celebrate.

A couple of years after Melissa died, we found someone who was able to melt down a pair of her favorite hoop earrings and make two small, simple rings from the remaining material, almost like wedding bands. We gave one to each of our daughters, and they wear theirs every day, everywhere they go. It's a reminder to celebrate their sister and live in the promised hope of being with her again some day.

Melissa's husband, Thomas, let Dayle borrow several journals and little notebooks of hers that were kept in a bedside drawer. Some of the entries are little prayers, things she wrote while living through a really good, much more stable patch of life. Other pages contain some of her less pleasant, more agitated thoughts. But there's enough to cherish in those few diaries that they bring great comfort to Dayle's heart, assuring her of Melissa's love for the Lord and her desire to trust Him with her struggles. It gives my wife cause to celebrate.

Allison, the only one of our immediate family who still lives in the town we all once did, takes new flowers to Melissa's grave at each change of the seasons. New ones again on her birthday.

"Instead of a present, I bring her flowers," she says. It's a lonely task in many ways. You may know her feelings exactly, perhaps being the one in your own family who cares for this loving detail. And while visiting the cemetery does often come with a dreary sense of empty longing, it remains a dutiful act of true devotion. An honor to their memory. A celebration of your relationship together and the privilege of having this person as part of who you are, as part of your life.

Laura keeps a box—a "memory box," she calls it—in the top of her closet. It holds a variety of little items that keep her heart tied to her sister's. A scarf Melissa wore. A pair of leather gloves. A copy of her funeral brochure. The last birthday gift she bought her. The last birthday card she *received* from her. A smocked bib Melissa sent to her son. A few other things as well, too special to mention. But her favorite collectible of all is something no one can ever see. Not even her. She's so worried about losing it, in fact, she keeps the box closed tight except for very brief moments—days when she's having a particularly hard time and needs just a taste of it to remind her. It's Melissa's smell. A hint of perfume and personality that's hard to describe and yet is uniquely hers. Some would think it invokes a noticeable whiff of sadness in the room. And it surely does. But the memories it exudes are worth millions an ounce to a loving survivor. It's the aroma of rich celebration.

I want to be able to celebrate more. I want to be able to listen to the CD of her testimony and celebrate the love God had shown her, how she battled through that cancer, how she could light up a room with the sheer vim of her presence. I want to be able to listen to the audio of her memorial service and celebrate her new life in her new home in heaven. I want to be able to swallow whole the full weight of my sadness over Melissa's death but soothe it down with enough gratitude and celebration till my face lights up the way a proud father's does . . . because I *am* one.

I not only want to *possess* and *preserve* her memory; I want to *celebrate* her memory.

Let's learn to celebrate.

It heals us.

Healing Unexpectedly

A good while before her death, Melissa received a phone call, quite out of the blue—someone asking if we and Melissa would be willing to come meet with them, with their family. An unusual request.

We had met them only briefly before but had never communicated directly with them again before this single phone contact. But we knew them. Oh, yes, we knew them. Knew exactly who they were. And knew something special about them.

Melissa said she'd go, so we arranged a meeting place near a halfway point between our respective homes—a Starbucks coffee shop we were both familiar with—and scheduled an appointment with them on what turned out to be a beautiful South Carolina Saturday.

We were all a bit tentative and nervous, I think, as we drove up. Excited. Edgy. Eager. Tense. The push and pull of competing emotions yanked and tugged at us in all directions, releasing butterflies that flitted within our stomachs and (from the feel of it) were trying to escape through our windpipes. Didn't know if they were leaving any room down there for coffee and Danish.

But we weren't really in town to sample the restaurant fare. A tall cup of blond roast was the farthest thing from my mind. We were there for something that wasn't on the menu but had been on our wish list for many years, never really imagining we'd actually be given the chance to enjoy.

To meet Melissa's son.

What a day! What an unexpected joy it was—and has been—for his adoptive mom and dad to invite us into his life. And to give us a living, breathing expression of Melissa to know, to give presents, to take on a beach vacation, to celebrate as one of our grandsons.

"Gabriel"—I'll call him Gabriel—is a quite unexpected cause for celebration. We're careful, of course, to monitor the level of contact we choose or are allowed to spend with him. We are extremely sensitive to maintain boundaries that protect his parents, his security, and his sense of identity in his rightful home and family. But I don't know how to thank our generous God enough for the opportunity to reconnect with this young fellow we had held at birth, as a newborn, never expecting in a million years to see him again in our human lifetime. And now when he hugs his granddaddy's neck, it feels almost like an embrace from heaven. Like a touch from my Melissa. That day in the hospital those many years ago, as she was delivering her only child, God was already healing me. It's just the way He does it. It's just how much He loves.

I understand this is a unique, unusual blessing God has given us—the opportunity to interact with Melissa's flesh and blood in this surprising, unexpected way. Practically a one-of-a-kind improbability. I still can't get over it.

But I am just hopeful enough in Christ to believe that He could amaze you as well with some kind of personalized assignment or opportunity that keeps your relationship with your lost loved one a renewed, renewing celebration.

I pray you'll keep looking for these unexpected forms of healing.

Dayle, for example, after looking and praying for a new, worthy outlet of her time, learned about the need for volunteers at our local crisis pregnancy center. She's been serving there in various ways for some time now but most recently mentoring young women who are in the same situation as our Melissa once was—scared, worried, lonely, needing hope and encouragement.

"Wouldn't you be really happy, Melissa, about what I'm doing here?" she imagines herself asking sometimes. I know she'd be smiling because she knows that her God—the One whose face is even now directly before her eyes—has been working out these various plans of healing in His masterful way all along. Melissa can turn to Him right now, right where she is, and say "thank You" for taking such good care of us.

The same way He's taking care of you.

As long as you're looking to Christ, He will continue to draw you onward along the path of healing. In those vast, dry places where you can't seem to walk and hold your head up at the same time, you can trust Him to do for you what you cannot do for yourself. And even if prayer seems futile and unnecessary, even if tears are quite often your only food—"day and night," as the psalmist said (Ps. 42:3)—hope still lives because God still loves.

For He crushes but also binds up; He strikes,
but His hands also heal.

JOB 5:18

——— ——— ———

A Letter to You

if you're contemplating suicide

I close with one very short, final note, eager to thank you for staying with me this long. I'm sure you know by now that much of my concern—for the rest of my life, I'm certain—involves spending time with people who, like you, are grappling with the tangled issues that make death seem preferable to living. My prayer for you is that you'll see death for the seduction it is.

We have invested this entire book walking through some of the further complications that are raised and left behind by suicide. They are enormous and never-ending. But even though ministering to the heart of other suicide survivors like me has been my chief goal in writing, I'm aware that the complications you feel in contemplating such an act are worthy of great care and time from others. You are not alone in your thinking, nor should you be left alone to wage this battle all by yourself.

I don't know that I really expect you to feel motivated or deterred away from suicide for fear of creating heartbreak in others. Your own problems likely feel large enough to you already, without adding any more worries on top of them. This is understandable. So here in my last appeal to you: instead of focusing on the challenges faced by families who lose a loved one to suicide, I ask you simply to consider a matter we touched on in this last chapter—how much there is to *celebrate* . . . about *you*.

As much as I miss my little Melissa, and as much as I long to see her again in heaven, I am working hard at moving through my grief, learning day by day (as I mentioned before) not only to survive her loss but to celebrate her life.

I admit, there will always be a little hollowness in those attempts. She did give us plenty of memorable material with which to recall her fondly, and I try to use well these scenes and snapshots as a means of honoring her and exalting God's healing mercies in our family. But hints of sadness will always streak my experiences, even in celebrating my precious firstborn.

Your friends and family members, however, need not mingle their love for you with memories alone but are still able to celebrate the person you are right now. These moments are still alive and more full of promise than you realize. Your relationships with these individuals may be strained and difficult, perhaps in very significant ways, but I'll still bet they could easily come up with a highlight reel of happier times with you, as well as their hopes for many more.

You are precious and special, my friend. Loved of God and bought at great price by the supreme sacrifice of His Son. You are unique and irreplaceable. And completely worthy of celebration. Let the people around you help you see this. It is more true than you know.

There is so much—*so very much*—to live for.

> *I have written you this brief letter . . . to testify that this is the true grace of God. Take your stand in it!*
> 1 PETER 5:12

EPILOGUE

Peace

$\mathcal{M}$ elissa struggled her whole life to be at peace. But she was rarely if ever at peace. And while I don't even yet understand all the reasons why contentment so deftly eluded her or why we could never decode the secret to help her gain victory over her challenges and circumstances, we do know this one blessed thing: she is now finally at peace.

It's hardly the way we would have wished it. (What an understatement.) It was wrong. It was illogical. Peace was *here*. She could have known it. We loved her. *Everybody* loved her. Even now people come up to me and tell me how sweet she was to them, how kindly she treated them, how much fun she was, how much they miss her. *Peace and joy were all around you, Melissa.* I wish so desperately she could have seen it.

But sitting where I am today, I must be willing to accept what has happened. It's horrible, but it's real. The only thing worse—if I can imagine it—would be not having the assurance that she at least did find what she was looking for.

Our Melissa is at peace.

Knowing God as Father and Savior, I have no problem believing that when He saw her spiraling, cascading, falling into that pit of depression and despondency, reaching out for what seemed her last, struggling appeal for help, He reached down, grabbed hold of her, and said, "Come on home, I've got you now." And at once, as Scripture says, she was "absent from the body . . . present with the Lord" (2 Cor. 5:8 KJV).

Finally, finally at peace.

Whatever the particular circumstance that brought you all the way through and to the end of this book, I hope, if nothing else, I've been able to leave you with a certain sense of peace. There's not much good about what's happened to us or about what's happening to you right now. Much of it is painful and evil, a gross mutation of what life was supposed to be like for us. I'm not prepared—and neither should *you* be—to think we won't carry this scar with us to the end of our days.

But I am prepared to find peace. The peace of God.

And I know by His grace that it is our guaranteed inheritance.

So let us step into this river of peace—bravely, willingly—undaunted by the swiftness of the current and the unknowns of the passage ahead.

Confident in Him, and committed to the generations that follow us, let us show what the glory of God looks like when it's shining across the shattered prisms of our jagged, broken heart. It just might give someone else the encouragement to keep going. It might even save another's life. And if we let Him, this river can take us and our families to a port of safety and settledness we thought we'd likely never see again.

Peace.

APPENDIX

A Word to Pastors

*I*f you're a pastor reading this book, looking for help in ministering to persons within your ministry and influence who are struggling with suicidal thoughts or recovering from a loved one's suicide, I feel compelled to summarize a few words of brotherly counsel. As a pastor for more than thirty-five years, and obviously as someone who's been touched by suicide at one of the most personal of levels, I understand the struggles on many sides of this sensitive issue. I've been there. So I feel confident these brief comments will prove effective as the Spirit works through both you and your sensitive prayers for people in this disturbing, disorienting crisis.

1. Be a learner. Each one of us has gleaned a great deal of knowledge from our studies, from our experience, from our time spent in Scripture. But you don't need to enter into the dynamics of suicide counseling pretending to know everything there is to know about it. You can still exude confidence without claiming to hog all the answers. No one on this side of eternity can fully understand or articulate the complex nature and theological mysteries surrounding the horrible act of suicide nor of the loss of rational thought that typically leads up to it. Grow your observations, increase your insights, but don't place pressure on yourself to grasp it all or to promise the absolute answer to every question.

2. *Be slow to offer platitudes or trite statements.* Stay quick with Scripture but sparing with human philosophy. I may be old-fashioned, but I still believe the Word of God contains power in its core and utterance. When shared from a heart of love, the Lord can use it to initiate deep healing and encouragement—and even the power to confront. You and I can each relate to the sensitive balance required of a counselor, navigating between gentleness and firmness as we help persons deal with their difficulties. Whenever we feel hesitant in being more direct and to the point, we can turn to the Bible for authority—not only over *them* but over *us*. Giving generalized, patchwork advice doesn't really do any good for anybody. It feels bad coming out; it feels tasteless going in.

3. *Provide a safe place for hurting people.* The pastor ought to be one who never judges and always loves. People who are suffering need to know they'll receive welcome and acceptance in a pastor's heart. This is not to say, again, that issues such as suicide don't often demand some words of serious challenge and blunt honesty. But even in doing so, we must continually remember our key responsibility is to love unconditionally,

continuing to care for them no matter what happens next in their lives and their subsequent choices.

4. *Teach people how to gain control of their thoughts.* The primary area where spiritual warfare takes place, we know, is the mind. We must keep before people the important warning and appeal of Romans 12:2: "Do not be conformed to this age, but be transformed by the renewing of your mind, so that you may discern what is the good, pleasing, and perfect will of God." I encourage you to refer back to the "Seven Steps to Spiritual Victory" outlined in chapter 3, using them in tandem with the strategies you have personally developed throughout your ministry in helping people concentrate on the things of God. Teach them to memorize Scripture. Lead them to think of God's Word as a healing, comforting place.

5. *Teach proper theology.* The largest singular religious group in our culture teaches that suicide is a mortal sin, one which immediately dooms its perpetrators/victims to hell. Clearly this is inconsistent with the teaching of Scripture. The Bible never makes such a declaration. Those who die in the Lord as believers are ushered into His kingdom no matter how their mortal life ends. Confront such blatant examples of improper theology and teach the truth of God's Word.

6. *Model appropriate behavior in relating to persons who have experienced suicide.* Something a suicide survivor quickly learns to recognize in conversation is when people who were acquainted with your deceased loved one are deliberately not talking about them—not because they're meaning to offend but because they're trying not to bring up a painful subject. The truth is, their silence hurts even more—as if we're all just

supposed to pretend now, despite how much a part of your life this person remains, that their memory is a taboo subject. It is politeness gone into unintentional pain infliction. One of the blessings you can be to them as a pastor is to speak of their departed person in your shared conversations—not all the time but at least occasionally. Seeing your ease and comfort in doing so, giving them permission to talk freely about the one they loved, serves a key role in their ongoing healing. Some cases could be different, of course, but you generally aid your ministry to them by not being embarrassed to say what you're probably already thinking anyway.

7. Learn about mental illness. The church many times has been woefully inadequate in reaching out to persons who either experience mental illness themselves or are dealing with it in their families. This lack of understanding and acceptance can cause many people to feel uncared for and separated from meaningful fellowship. And when we as pastors, not in dismissiveness perhaps but at least in ignorance, give them "snap out of it" advice (or something in that family of faulty counsel), we do more harm than good. Are there spiritual aspects to mental illness that can be dealt with in the usual manner for experiencing healthy Christian growth—prayer, discipline, church involvement, Scripture use and memory? Yes, of course. But that's not the only thing involved. More than ever—if you intend to serve your congregation well—you need a working knowledge of what causes mental illness and depression and how to assist its sufferers with the best kind of loving assistance.

Persons who are suicidal come to their despondent

conclusions from all kinds of places—situational causes, relational failure, long history with depression and anxiety. As mentioned earlier, you cannot expect to uncover every root and know exactly what to say in every circumstance. But you are wise and caring to seek out people you trust in the medical and psychiatric fields who can help you spot the signals that give you direction toward how best to serve the suicidal.

You will be most successful in ministering to both the suicidal and their survivors if you model for them a level of transparency that assures them *you're* not perfect either. People tend to relax and feel more comfortable opening up with church leaders who don't hide their own struggles and deficiencies.

Please hear me, however—this swing of the pendulum must be held in balance. As surely as people need to see you as a real person, they also need to hear you saying, "Here's what the Lord has done for me." "Here's the Scripture that brought me out of my malaise." "Here's the godly counsel I heard that really helped me in dealing with this." Ask the Lord for help in modeling both transparency and responsibility, all at the same time.

I hope, if He has touched your heart in a particularly strong way throughout the course of this book, and if you can see in your own ministry the great need for attending to these significant realities in your congregation and community, that you and I can talk further in the days ahead. I would welcome that. I would love to hear what you are seeing and learning, as well as to share with you anything else from our experience that might be helpful to you—to ask each other questions, to explore

God's Word in even greater detail on this matter. Please visit me at frankpage.org so we can continue to learn and dialogue together.

God bless you in your work and service to Him, His people, and His kingdom.

About the Author

$\mathcal{F}$rank Page is president and CEO of the Southern Baptist Convention Executive Committee, and is known across the country and world for his personable, proven leadership. Having served as a pastor for more than three decades, he has twice led churches through seasons of growth that doubled their original size, creating missions and ministries that continue to impact their local communities and beyond. He holds a Bachelor of Science degree in psychology and counseling from Gardner Webb University, as well as the Master of Divinity and Ph.D. from Southwestern Baptist Theological Seminary. He and his wife, Dayle, reside near Nashville, Tennessee. They have three daughters—Melissa, Laura, and Allison—as well as three grandsons.